What Every Successful Woman Knows

12 Breakthrough Strategies to Get the Power and Ignite Your Career

JANICE REALS ELLIG

WILLIAM J. MORIN

McGraw-Hill

NEW YORK   CHICAGO   SAN FRANCISCO   LISBON   LONDON
MADRID   MEXICO CITY   MILAN   NEW DELHI   SAN JUAN
SEOUL   SINGAPORE   SYDNEY   TORONTO

Library of Congress Cataloging-in-Publication Data

Ellig, Janice Reals.
    What every successful woman knows : 12 breakthrough strategies to get the power
and ignite your career / Janice Reals Ellig and William J. Morin.
        p. cm.
    Includes bibliographical references.
    ISBN 0-07-136996-1
    1. Women executives.   2. Businesswomen—Promotions.   3. Career
development.   I. Morin, William J.   II. Title.

HD6054.3 .E43 2001
650.14'082—dc21
                                                                                    00-068697

McGraw-Hill

A Division of The **McGraw·Hill** *Companies*

1 2 3 4 5 6 7 8 9 0 AGM/AGM 0 9 8 7 6 5 4 3 2 1

ISBN 0-07-136996-1

Printed and bound by Quebecor/Martinsburg.

McGraw-Hill books are available at special quantity discounts to use as premiums and
sales promotions, or for use in corporate training programs. For more information,
please write to the Director of Special Sales, Professional Publishing, McGraw-Hill, Two
Penn Plaza, New York, NY 10121-2298. Or contact your local bookstore.

This book is printed on recycled, acid-free paper containing a minimum of
50% recycled, de-inked fiber.

Dedication

To my sister Adrienne, a career woman ahead of her time, who gave me inspiration and courage . . .

To my husband, Bruce, a true soulmate, who gives me love as well as friendship . . .

To my daughter, Meredith, who gives my life wholeness and new meaning.

Janice Reals Ellig

To Nicole, my first grandchild, who was born on the very day Janice and I finished this book. *May you define your own success and have as much of it as you desire.*

William J. Morin

Contents

Foreword

Some four decades have passed since the women's liberation movement of the 1960s catapulted women into the corporate workplace and changed the face of corporate America forever. One would think that by this time, there ought to be no need for a book like *What Every Successful Woman Knows: 12 Breakthrough Strategies to Get the Power and Ignite Your Career*. But there is. Emphatically, there is.

In fact, this book by two very savvy business observers comes at a pivotal time—and not a moment too soon. For the work world is changing almost as fast as the world in general, and women's place in both is changing as well. As the "third generation" of women begins to take its place in corporate America, they confront very different challenges from those faced by the first and second generations: different economic realities, different management needs, and to some extent, different attitudes on the part of their male colleagues. They are also finding, of course, as this lively and engaging book makes clear, that in far too many cases, the attitudes of male colleagues are not different enough.

Where the first generation of books for and about corporate women justified or proclaimed their right to play a role in corporate America, and the second provided essential advice about how to do the job well and blend into the landscape, Janice Reals Ellig and William J. Morin here tell corporate women what we need to know

now—how to get and use the personal and organizational tools that can widen the opportunities available to us and help us move into positions of power.

I am part of the second generation of corporate women. I spent eleven years toiling in the vineyards of Gannett & Co., Inc. before being named President and CEO of *USA WEEKEND* magazine, the nation's second largest publication. Like a lot of my women CEO colleagues, I suppose I thought that achieving the chief-executive title would be the start of smooth sailing in terms of the work itself; I also thought it would mean I had conquered all the problems of being a woman in the workforce. I was wrong on both counts—which is why I am a CEO who is studying for her MBA and why I wish I had had *What Every Successful Woman Knows* at the start of my career.

Reals Ellig and Morin have produced a useful, practical guide not just to navigating the currents of the corporate workplace but to commanding the ship. Their "doable dozen" breakthrough strategies are eminently *actionable,* and they're presented in a common-sense way. Why didn't I think about planning my career the same way I think about creating a business plan? Why don't women in general bring to their careers the same exquisite planning skills they tend to bring to planning their weddings? Why don't we take on a wide scope of management skills with the same comprehensiveness we bring to learning about our children's educational options? Why don't we picture what we want from the career, prioritize, and problem-solve with the same near-ruthless focus we bring to running a household or raising children, and go after the responsibility and the power? *We know how to do this,* and *What Every Successful Woman Knows* puts it all in perspective, gets us to home in on what's needed for success, and what's more, gets us to put it on paper.

The twelve strategies here are more than advice; they're an agenda, and it's one I think every working woman can profit from following. How sensible to read that you must picture what you want if you're going to get it . . . that you really have to fit into your corporate culture, so you had better pick a company whose culture you can fit into comfortably . . . that going for P&L responsibility is an essential step—a lesson this die-hard liberal arts major learned late in life. I heartily recommend the book's exercises and tips—like those for getting your political antennae in working order. Company politics are inevitable, and women must be comfortable with that fact. I like the reminder that women spend time trying to help others rather than trying to figure out who can help them. As a journalist in a journalism organization, I particularly appreciate the book's lessons in communicating briefly and succinctly. And as a woman, I value the fact that the book is co-authored by a woman and a man. Men and women working together is simply the way the world is. Men and women working together as cogently as Morin and Reals Ellig have done in this book is the way the world should be.

Opportunities bring with them responsibilities. As a woman, and specifically as a woman boss, I believe it is my responsibility to make the workplace as fair and as rewarding as possible for *all* the players. But I also believe I have a special responsibility to helping working women seize their opportunities. As business and human development experts whose insights are widely respected, Janice and Bill have taken seriously their responsibility to deepen our understanding of how corporate women can make the most of the opportunities available to them. The advice, ideas, and wisdom they offer in *What Every Successful Woman Knows: 12 Breakthrough Strategies to Get the Power and Ignite Your Career* can make a big difference to women, to men, and to corporate workplaces everywhere.

Marcia Bullard
President and CEO,
USA WEEKEND magazine

Acknowledgments

Writing *What Every Successful Woman Knows* has been a highly collaborative process, and we are pleased to acknowledge the assistance and input we have received from so many quarters.

First and foremost, we are grateful to the hundreds of successful women interviewed for the book. They offered us their intelligence, insight, and candor. The experiences they shared with us are the core of *What Every Successful Woman Knows;* there would be no book without them. Many of them wished to remain anonymous, but we would like to acknowledge Heidi Schneider, Marilyn Puder-York, Jewelle Bickford, Gail Blanke, Judy Haberkorn, Christina Gold, Bernadette Kenny, Kathy Dore, Marcia Bullard, Julie Johnson Reid, Ann Kaplan, Carol Taber, Marcy Syms, Ann Reese, Janet Green, Gail Natoli, Nina Smith, Candy Straight, Marilyn Goldstein, Kathy Boyle, Nancy Amiel, Marianne Toldalagi, Marti Dinerstein, Irene Cohen, Jane King, Christine Nolte, Cristine Cronin, Jeri Sedlar, Sandy Helton, Davia Temin, Carole Hyatt, and Edie Weiner.

We are of course grateful to our wonderful agent, Sally Wecksler, and to the professionals at McGraw-Hill: editors Betsy Brown and Kelli Christiansen for their thoughtfulness, encouragement, and reasoned insights, senior editing supervisor Scott Amerman for his guidance in editing from manuscript to bound book, and Publisher/Editor-in-Chief Jeffrey Krames for his support and enthusiasm. Special thanks to our editorial collaborator, Susanna Margolis, who helped us crystallize our thinking and express it clearly and "strategically," and to Dr. Tessa Warschaw, who found Susanna for us.

Both of us are grateful to early bosses who mentored our own corporate careers. Interestingly, Bill wishes to acknowledge two women executives who supported him early in his career, Pat Neighbors of Avon, and Betty Duval of Dow Jones, while Janice thanks two men in her professional life, Phil Lassiter and Jamie McLane, for the opportunity to have "a seat at the table" and for the chance to learn the lessons that prompted this book. Janice also acknowledges her sister, Elaine Williams Hunt, one of corporate America's highly successful women, for her encouragement and for inspiring all women who have a family first and a career next.

Finally, we want to express our thanks to each other. Friends for twenty years, we found in the writing of this book that our separate perspectives were even more enriching than we had suspected. We believe our collaboration is an example of the success that can be achieved when men and women work together on an equal basis. Shared power, we have found, is power well used. When corporate America truly unleashes that resource, it will thrive even more.

INTRODUCTION

Where Are Women Now?

In a letter written more than 200 years ago, Abigail Adams famously chided her husband to "remember the ladies" in framing the Constitution and to "give us more rights." The nation's eventual second president was quick to respond. "Oh, Abigail dear," said John Adams, "the men would never give up their masculine privilege!"

Across corporate America, too many men at the top are clinging to their masculine privilege with all the fervor of anointed princes upholding a sacred prerogative and fighting off a palace coup. They treat the executive suite like a men's club. Only club members are admitted; only club members can make the real corporate decisions and wield the real corporate authority.

This is not good for business.

It is the twenty-first century, and in corporate America, the guys in suits are almost as likely to be women as men. Tailored or Ann Taylored, casually chic or fashionably formal, equipped with their cell phones and Palm Pilots, their MBA degrees and *WSJ* subscriptions, their sleek laptops and overstuffed briefcases, wherever the business elite meet, women are there.

1

You see them in the corridors of gleaming office towers. They're lunching at the "in" restaurant in the business district. They're plugged in at the VIP lounges of major airports . . . working out in the business hotel gym . . . phoning from 37,000 feet to leave yet another set of instructions for the team members they direct.

And they're not just running public relations anymore, or human resources, those traditional arenas to which women were invariably assigned. They're not just writing the house newsletter or the press release, either. Instead, they're headlining in it—with assignments in just about every area of corporate life and just about every kind of job. From general management to finance, strategic planning to quality control, front to middle to back office, women are everywhere in corporate America.

Except for one place: the seat of power. The Chairman's Table. The inner sanctum where strategic policy issues are raised, discussed, and decided. With only a few exceptions, there's still a big, thick, heavy door keeping women from a seat at that table. And the sign on the door still reads "Men Only."

PAINTING THE PICTURE BY THE NUMBERS

No, this is not "yet another" whining, carping complaint about how women are kept in an inferior place in our society. It is a reality check. As we write this book, in the autumn of 2000, three facts alone paint a picture of that reality:

1. Only two of the Fortune 500 companies are headed by women— Hewlett-Packard by Carly Fiorina and Avon by Andrea Jung.

2. Only 83 women versus 2,267 men hold positions in the highest ranks of corporate America—the clout titles of chairman, CEO, vice chairman, president, COO, SEVP, and EVP.

3. Women hold only 2.7 percent of the top-earner spots in the Fortune 500—63 positions out of 2,320.

It's no coincidence: When you are locked out of the policy-making arena, you are effectively cut off from a range of opportunities and from the compensation such opportunities command.

Has there been progress? Certainly:

- In 1995, fewer than 10 percent of board members in the Fortune 500 companies were women. By 1999, women held 11.2 percent of the seats.

- In 1996, 10 percent of corporate officers were women—20 percent of those in line positions. By 1999, 11.9 percent of corporate officers were women—with 27.5 percent of them holding line jobs.

- In 1980, for every dollar earned by white men in corporate America, white women earned 65 cents, African-American women earned 59 cents, and Hispanic women earned 55 cents. By 1998, white women were earning 78 cents for every dollar earned by white men, African-American women were earning 67 cents, and Hispanic women were earning 56 cents.[1]

Progress, yes—but painfully slow progress. For the women living it, it's a dismal story and a painful one.

More than eighty years after having won the right to vote, women are still struggling to succeed in the corporate world. And as women's capabilities and relevant expertise increase, so does the frustration they're experiencing. We're hearing it over and over again, from capable, high-performance women on the corporate front lines, and the message is almost always the same:

The opportunities just aren't being offered, we aren't moving up fast enough, and we're deeply angered. When we see less capable men getting the choicest positions and CEOs with poor corporate performance records being handsomely rewarded, the meritocracy value becomes meaningless. Where is the investment in us?

What's behind the lockout of women? According to a 1999 report from the Society of Human Resource Management,[2] the top five barriers to women's advancement in corporate America are: (1) a culture that favors men, (2) men's stereotyped preconceptions of women, (3) the lack of female representation on corporate boards, (4) women's exclusion from informal networks, and (5) management's perception—read "men's perception"—that family responsibilities will interfere.

These are not imaginary barriers. They really do prevent real people from achieving their potential and seizing opportunities that should be open to them. By the very nature of the corporate pyramid, senior-level opportunities in the corporate world are few and far between. If you're fortunate enough to be a woman near the summit, you're very much alone, and you know it.

ECONOMIC REALITY, BUSINESS ESSENTIAL

Progress on this front is essential. We'll say it again: Locking women out of the top of the corporate pyramid is bad for business. That's why it *should be* the concern of every board director, executive, manager, senior officer, and leader in corporate America. In fact, those corporate leaders who haven't yet figured out the business case for diversity—not just in the workplace but in the executive suite—may not deserve to be corporate leaders at all. The lockout isn't serving shareholder value, it isn't serving employees, and it certainly isn't serving customers.

It is by now a truism that women control some 80 percent of the $3 trillion spent annually by U.S. consumers and that they manage the finances in nearly three-quarters of American households. Is your company planning to market to these women? If so, it would be a good idea to have a few of them in seats of power to provide insight and understanding to the decision-making process and to reflect the company's commitment to this important target market.

And just who is your company planning to hire over the next few years? The war for talent rages on, and the future need for executive, administrative, and managerial occupations is projected to far exceed average employment growth. Services, wholesale and retail trade, finance, insurance, and real estate are expected to lead the way in their appetite for people—especially people with computer skills, specialized technical training, or graduate study. Where will companies find the human resources they need if they systematically continue to keep women out of power?

And where do the male leaders of American corporations think those women go? Cut off at the pass, kept from the real power, tolerated but not totally accepted, an astonishing percentage of them start their own businesses. In fact, many of the best and brightest women are opting out of corporations in alarming numbers and are launching companies in record numbers. In 1977, there were 0.7 million women-owned firms in this country; ten years later, there were 4.1 million; and in 1999, there were 9.1 million. Nearly 30 percent of women business owners with prior private-sector experience cited the glass ceiling as the reason they left to start their own business: 47 percent said their contributions were not recognized or valued; 34 percent said they were not taken seriously; 29 percent said they felt isolated; and 27 percent cited seeing others promoted while they were not as the reasons for getting out of the corporation into their own businesses.

In other words, the woman you lock out of the executive suite today may become your competitor tomorrow.

Diversity is an economic reality and therefore a business essential in today's global, digital economy. In a globally competitive world, a world in which, as Hewlett-Packard's Fiorina has said, companies are "competing hard to win every day," survivability changes the power equation very quickly.

5

BET ON THE BOARDS

SCENARIO:

At a dinner following a board meeting, an external board member asked the chairman why he was not able to find a qualified female director. "I've been looking for five years now," he replied, "ever since we went public, yet each candidate I see lacks something. And I'll be damned if I'm going to compromise my standards just to have a woman on the board." The female finance director, hearing this exchange, looked around the table at the all-male board and thought but did not say: "Won't compromise your standards? You already have." A true story—it took another three years before a woman was added to the board.

Corporate boards are key to opening the doors to women, and today, with 87 percent of Fortune 1000 companies boasting at least one female board member, and with more and more women in the ranks of shareholders, we're beginning to see them as sources of change. At annual meetings, both women and men shareholders are asking questions about the diversity of the senior management staff and the board of directors; those questions need better answers than most corporations are able to give today.

Over time, we believe corporate boards not only will push their CEOs to add more women directors but also will look more closely at the career paths of women—and minorities—within the corporation. If such scrutiny shows that high-potential women and minorities in middle and senior management positions are not moving up—or are bailing out of the corporation—more boards will be asking why. They will be looking closely at the quality of the women who leave and not just the quantity. If they find that it is the best talent that has been recruited away or that has left to start up their own business, as has often been the case, they will question the male executives in charge of the company and responsible for developing its future leadership. These questions can be a potent spur to progress.

A door that is held ajar just-so-far-and-no-farther for women is no way to ensure diversity. On the contrary. It's a good way to inflame the frustration women have felt for too long. For complacent or backward corporations that continue to keep an iron wall between women and corporate power, the handwriting is on that wall.

GLASS CEILING, IRON WALL

It is the iron wall that is holding up the glass ceiling, and it's nothing new. As far back as 1992, Stanford labor economist Myra H. Strober noted that "wall" was "just a new name for an old phenomenon called occupational segregation. . . . Jobs get segregated when women begin to move through them," Ms. Strober said. "That's just a way of maintaining old types of discrimination."[3] Women may chip away at the glass ceiling as much as they want—they may even crash through it—but until the wall is removed, they won't have entry into the seat of power.

If you're a woman, you feel the cold face of this iron wall every day. You didn't get the title; instead you got a pat on the back from the boss and a sympathetic, whispered exhortation to "hang in there." Or you've got the title, but you notice you're still not part of the inner circle. Or you've made it into the inner circle, but the man beside you gets to run the choice project while you're asked to handle the administrative trivia or continue to run your usual operation.

The iron wall is in your face. Until you scale it, you will continue to lose out on compensation, choice assignments, and opportunity for the highest stages of career development. Until women are over the wall, through the door, and empowered to call the shots from their own seat at the table, they will continue to find their ambitions unfulfilled, their potential leashed, and their careers, in a very real sense, on hold.

The answer is power. To get it, you're going to have to go after it like a hunter out to bag the big game. You'll need the right equipment, the right training, the right support, and the desire to get it. You'll need to hone your corporate savvy and your navigational skills. This book can be your guide.

THE CORPORATE WOMAN'S POWER AGENDA

Power is the goal. Strategy is the means to the goal. To be precise: twelve strategies. These are practical, useful strategies, defined in practical, useful terms. Together, they form an action plan for going after your rightful place in the inner sanctum of corporate power. These twelve strategies comprise the corporate woman's power agenda. Here they are:

- Career Choices: Look Around to Go Forward
- Corporate Life: Fit In or Move On
- Risk-Taking: Be on the Line
- Senior Management: Lead and Feed the Boss
- Politics: Chat with the Boys and Get Elected
- Communications: Be Business-Wise and Business-Brief
- Marketing: Brand You!
- Responsibility: Be Significant, Dump the Insignificant
- Focus: Do the 80-20 Split
- Power: Be a General by Being a Generalist
- Sex: Take It or Leave It, but Control It
- Leadership: Be the Lead Dog; It's a Better View

How did we come up with these twelve strategies? "We" didn't. Rather, we consolidated the advice of the 200-plus corporate women interviewed for this book. They candidly revealed the successes and failures they've experienced in their careers, careers in which they've not only had to do the job for which they were hired but also had to bring a battering ram up against the barriers corporations put in their way. The women range in age from 35 to 60, represent all major industries, come from all regions of the country, and have all achieved senior levels in the corporate hierarchy. Many of their names are well known, not only to the readers of this book but to a wider, general audience. Yet in their view, none of these women has attained the full power and recognition they want and believe they deserve.

We have added to their wisdom the experience we ourselves have gained through the years across a number of industries. As you've gathered from our names on the cover, we are a man and a woman, and we bring to our task both our separate perspectives and the synergy of our collective experience. The woman among us has successfully attained executive leadership roles in a range of corporations and not-for-profit boards, while the man has not only run companies—including his own—but has also spent years coaching women and men in corporate leadership development.

Through the lens of this collective experience, we've crystallized the insights of the women interviewed for the book into the doable dozen strategies—an effective action plan for attaining the power in your organization and igniting your career.

If you feel stalled at the three-quarter mark of the race despite doing all the right things . . . if you're tired of standing in line dutifully as you watch men leapfrog ahead . . . if you're ready to boost yourself past the resistance and jump-start the next phase of your career, the doable dozen should be on your agenda. They have been tested, and they work. They can help you take your place among the real decision-makers, assume a role in determining policy, have a say in corporate strategy. They can help put you on the track that leads to the chairman's floor, preferably to his office, eventually to his job—if that is what you want.

Are you ready?

Let's go get the power.

Career Choices: Look Around to Go Forward

Bill: I think there is real danger in aiming strictly for power. It may ultimately not be good for your life or your career.

Janice: That goes for men as well as women. For women, the issue is that getting to the top often means they have to do even more than men. This means putting in extra face-time as well as producing epic results. To get ahead, we often become workaholics—or today, e-holics.

Bill: But tunnel vision can make you miss a lot—including the target. And I mean that for men as well. Corporate power is not just about work; a corporate leader plays many roles.

Janice: Professional demands, personal demands, community activities: It means that the women who seek top corporate spots have to be highly focused and integrate their lives. The question is, to women—and men—do you really want a power position in a corporation? If the answer is yes, then all should have a fair shot at getting it.

Far too often, the senior women we interviewed for this book lamented that by most measurements, especially among other women, they had attained title and wealth but still did not feel successful or satisfied. All agreed that their career target needed to be something more than title and money. Many felt the price for success was too high. Others wished they had thought more thoroughly about what was important and had seen themselves married to life and not simply to a job.

Some had been running so long and so hard in the corporate world they had forgotten why they wanted it or found it was no longer fun. Several of these women had stayed in positions to get to the top and once there found that it wasn't their dream position after all. Women seem to reflect on where they are in their lives more than men. Is that healthy? We think so. We believe it's good to re-evaluate where you want to be going; otherwise, you may never get to your destination. That's why the first approach is to get clear about what you wish for; after all, you may get it.

FOUR STEPS

Where do you want to be in twenty years? ten years? even five years? You can read a book, take a workshop, hire a coach, or see a psychologist to try to figure out the answer to this question. Thousands of people do. All find that while it's often easy to know what you don't want, figuring out what you really do want is a lot tougher.

Step 1: Visualize Your Future.   Let's do some visualizing of your future. It is an exercise not unlike what senior teams do at management off-sites when they look at where they are, where they want to be, and how they are going to get there. For our purposes, we will treat this as a game—that is, we'll play by rules that are limited only by your imagination. Start by visualizing your dream future—an achievable wish, but a "stretch wish."

What's a stretch wish? One corporate woman tells how a persistent executive recruiter got her to stretch her professional ambitions beyond the position she had, a position in which she was quite happy.

The stretch impelled the executive to interview for the position that in turn led her to significant leadership at a new company.

So let's begin by stretching the imagination and reaching for your achievable dream. Try this exercise: Write an article for *Fortune* magazine on the subject of you five years from now. What will you have accomplished? What will people say about you? What will you have done in your community and with your family? Focus on the following to get a complete picture for this article.

1. How much power or influence do you have over other people? How many and what kind of people seek your advice?

2. How well known are you? Who is in your circle of power?

3. What makes you unique? What is your brand image? How do people differentiate you from others?

4. What is your net worth?

   $500,000

   1,000,000

   3,000,000

   6,000,000

   8,000,000

   10,000,000

   15,000,000

   20,000,000 or more

5. Describe in detail what you are doing in terms of:
   - Your career (are you CEO, Division Head, President, COO, Director—or have you left the corporate world to pursue other interests?)
   - Your personal life
     - Spouse/partner
     - Children

- Special interests: Charities, not-for-profit boards, foundations, corporate boards, vocations, other activities (writing, painting, sports)

These questions tell you about the tangible and materialistic aspects of the future you seek. Now try to imagine what you will feel once you attain that future, and describe this in your *Fortune* article.

6. Describe the sense of joy and exhilaration you feel in your moment of achievement. What do people applaud? What are you most proud of?

7. Describe your sense of well-being.

   - Are you excited about life?
   - Do you feel you're having a positive impact on others?
   - Are you happy?
   - Do you have a passion for what you're doing?
   - Is each day an exciting challenge you enjoy confronting?

Now step back from this look at the future and articulate the five key steps that got you to your moment of achievement and your sense of well-being. These steps are nothing less than a strategy to get you to where you want to be.

For example, suppose your article saw you as the CEO of an e-commerce business. Looking back from your moment of achievement, you can see that what was essential to that achievement was that you did the following: (1) made two strategic career moves to e-commerce companies to get the exposure and experience you needed; (2) joined several associations that put you in front of significant people in this business; (3) took a number of related leadership seminars that gave you the expertise—and contacts—to help you build your business; (4) attended an international conference on the business and hooked up with the movers and the shakers; and (5) got smart on a specific subject and became a regular speaker on the topic, with the publicity and contacts that found you the partner you needed to grow the business.

NASA played this game to get the United States to the moon. NASA scientists imagined standing on the moon with the equipment that got them there. They then were asked to design the equipment— as well as the steps it would take to get to the moon. As you define your picture, you can do the same.

Writing your *Fortune* article and identifying the five steps that brought you to your moment of achievement constitutes a challenging exercise. If you were able to project your goal and your sense of well-being—and how you would have gotten there—you're in good strategic shape. If not, the remaining strategies may help you realize your potential and get you to where you want to be.

Step 2: What Is Power—And Why Do You Want It? In *Fortune* magazine's October 2000 issue,[4] devoted to "The Power 50" among corporate women, Hewlett-Packard Chairman and CEO Carly Fiorina defines power as "the ability to change things;" in the words of another one of the 50, Fidelity Investments' Gail McGovern, it is "synonymous with influence." We agree. To attain power in an organization, a person has to take action, not just react—to seize control and exert influence, not just be a follower—to energize and motivate others, not just wait for orders. You can have power without a leadership position, but you can't get to a leadership position without power. This book is about acquiring power so that you can attain the leadership position you want.

But: Are you sure you *want* power? Not just think you *ought to* want power but *really* want it? As with getting married or starting a family, doing it because your friends have done it is not the right reason.

Judy Haberkorn *had* power; for many years, she was the President of the Consumer Group of what was then known as Bell Atlantic. Several months after her retirement, she told a group of women that only now did she realize that "for a long time, I was running on empty." She felt that she had been acting "like a wounded athlete, who kept going back into the game, working harder and longer to make the numbers," but rarely reaping the attendant rewards. In retrospect she wished she had put that effort into an enterprise that she ran and reflected her passion, succeeding or failing by and for herself.

That's why it's important to be sure before the fact that power is what you want. What do you aim to do with the power once you get it? Does power fit with the rest of your life? Will having power make you feel fulfilled? Gail Blanke, President of Lifedesigns, says it's essential to "answer the fundamental question: 'What are you committed to?' If you are committed to being a CEO, you have to ask the underlying question: to do what? I want to be a CEO so I can 'be this or that' or because it enables me to do 'this, that, or the other.' "

It's a little like another question Gail poses to women in her Lifedesigns workshop: "How many of you want to lose weight?" Every hand is raised in answer. "Of course," Gail remarks, "we all want to weigh less. And we know how to do it. But often we don't know why we want to lose weight." For Gail, for example, the regular workouts at Cardio Fitness are not just because she likes to exercise but because she has a vision: She pictures herself running on the beach in twenty years with her (yet to be born) grandchildren, looking and feeling great.

So when you look back to your *Fortune* magazine article, look to see what you have done with the power you achieved. Ask what you mean by power: Do you mean power over people, power over your own life, or having influence or impact? Define your terms.

Now let's see if you really want power in corporations.

We'll keep it really simple. If you answer yes to all five questions below, you probably want more power in your job. If you answer yes to three or fewer, rethink the corporate challenge you're willing to take on. Be honest. You'll only be cheating yourself if you're not.

1. I thrive on working in a competitive corporate environment.

2. I like calling the shots, being accountable, and sitting at the boss's table.

3. I am driven by the idea of a bigger title and more responsibility.

4. I need the rewards—money, recognition, visibility, and other perks—which I can get in a corporation.

5. I want to constitute my own brand within a successful company brand.

Step 3: Draw a Circle and Look Around It. What's the emphasis in your life? To find it, draw a circle—a pie that represents your waking hours, as in Figure 1.1. Now divide the pie into four slices: work, family, recreation, and community. *Recreation* refers to everything you do for yourself, and *community* means everything you do for others—whether it's volunteering at the local food pantry or hosting a fundraiser for the political candidate of your choice or mentoring a child who's having a tough time. Divide the pie honestly: How much of your time do you devote to each slice of your life? How are your waking hours segmented?

Of course, the slices will never be equal all the time. You may not want them to be. However, remember the old saw that nobody on his deathbed ever regretted not spending more time at the office.

If the biggest wedge of your pie is work, with only meager slivers offered to the rest of life, plan to make a change right away by asking yourself what's important in your life and doing something to pro-

Figure 1.1 Pie: How You Spend Your Waking Hours.

mote it *right this minute.* Go ahead. You can't remember the last time you and your husband, boyfriend, or friend spent a special evening? Call that person and make a date—and make the reservation. Call that woman who's been pestering you to volunteer for the 10K charity run and offer to man a refreshment station—*and* promise you'll show up at the organizing meeting. None of this will get you off the hook for the long haul, but as a first step toward reducing work's dominance in your life, it will give you a sense that the balance can be shifted and that you're in control. The organization will survive. We just think we are indispensable.

Remember the great AT&T commercial where the woman is about to leave for the office when her daughters, dressed in bathing suits and flippers, beg her to go to the beach. The mother gives in saying "OK, I'll do the meeting by phone from the beach." The scene changes to the two little girls playing at the beach; when the phone rings, the youngest squeals "It's time for the meeting," and we hear the song, "Girls just wanna have fun." How much fun are you having? Is the circle right for you? Your life may not be balanced due to all the work demands you have, but is it integrated enough so that the scene at the beach could be you?

Betsy Holden teaches Sunday school, does extensive volunteer work with impoverished kids in a tough Chicago neighborhood, and founded a group called the Working Mom's Exchange Network. She's a wife and the mother of two young children with whom she insists on spending plenty of time. She is also the CEO at Kraft Foods and thus the head of the nation's largest food packager.

Granted, Betsy Holden has a knack for organization. The real knack, however, is that she applies her organizational skills to integrating all aspects of her life into one organic whole. That's the lesson we want to impart: Balance your life and work by integrating what you do for a living with who you are and how you live your life as a human being. Balance is an elusive quality; integration is controllable.

Holden, according to an article about her in the *New York Times*,[5] "charted, listed, categorized and logically plotted not just her rise to power, but her family life." The volunteer organization with which she works is supported by the marketing community in Chicago, so working with it gives Holden a chance to teach young people and to network with clients and colleagues at the same time. Similarly, the Working Mom's Exchange Network was an organization Holden founded at Kraft when she first became a mother. The Network is a group of Kraft women who share the results of such assignments as researching preschools and writing wills.

In short, Holden found ways to make work and life *complement* one another, to unite her community activism and her professional outreach, her parenting and her organizational networking—even her power base–building. She didn't have to choose between getting a living and getting a life. There was no "between" there at all.

Holden can serve as a role model and object lesson as you work toward taking the slash out from between the words "work" and "life" in work/life balance. Find ways, as she did, to integrate work, family, recreation, and community. We know a high-ranking insurance company executive who talked her company into becoming a sponsor of an organization building housing for low-income families, then organized colleagues and clients to volunteer. Now, one weekend a month, the company sends a squadron of employees and their families, accompanied by squadrons of clients and their families, to help give something back to their community. That's work, family, recreation, and community all at once.

Not everything will be that straightforward or that all-encompassing, but it's the idea of integration that counts. Do you keep two appointment books, one for work and one for life? Toss them. Replace them with a single appointment calendar that you buy or create—whether on paper or on your computer or PDA. You have one life. Work is an important part of it, but make sure it is only one important part.

Step 4: What Is Important to You.   In another of author Bill Morin's books, the one on *Total Career Fitness,*[6] readers are asked to analyze what they want from their career. Let's use some of Bill's characteristics as well as some others, shown below, separated into four categories that relate to different aspects of most jobs. Completing the checklist will help you determine what is most important to you in your career.

Read through the whole list to answer this question: "At this time in my life, which do I want most right now?" Number each item in order of importance, from one through three, with one being the most important and three least important. (Remember that this is not an intellectual exercise; it is an emotional one.)

You should treat these as one long list. Limit your number-one selections to only ten items. Force yourself to rank the list into groups of ten (for example, ten number-one choices, ten number-twos, and ten number-threes). When you've finished, ignore the number-two and -three choices, at least for now. Then take your top ten, and select your top five.

Company characteristics

_____ Financial strength

_____ Company size

_____ Growth potential

_____ Corporate brand name

_____ Geographic location

_____ Corporate values (especially fairness, trust, etc.)

_____ Smart colleagues

_____ Good working conditions (cleanliness, safety, etc.)

_____ Friendly, open environment

_____ Family friendly policies

Job characteristics

_____ Title

_____ Supportive boss

_____ Opportunity for professional development

_____ Opportunity for personal development

_____ Opportunity to learn about other areas

_____ Clearly defined roles, responsibilities, expectations

_____ Authority to make or participate in decisions

_____ Office (size, number of windows, decor)

_____ Little travel

_____ Much travel

_____ Fun

_____ Challenging/interesting

_____ Easy to do

_____ Flexible schedule/telecommuting

Remuneration and advancement issues

_____ High salary

_____ Pay for performance/bonus opportunities

_____ Good profit-sharing, benefits, perks

_____ Good potential for advancement

_____ Recognition and reward opportunities

_____ Retirement benefits

Before interpreting your answers, you need to remember that in the real world, it's rare that anybody gets it all. If you are sincerely committed to gaining power and balance, you'll have to make some hard decisions about how you live.

SUMMARY

You've visualized your dream, determined why you want power, analyzed how you see yourself integrating your professional and personal life (not lives), and identified your top five career priorities. Now here are some tips to help you get to where you want to be.

Looking around to go forward: fifteen tips

1. Visualize what you really desire in the future.

2. Lay out the five key steps that you must take to make your dream a reality.

3. Make sure your dream is a stretch goal or desire, but doable.

4. Know what you are going to do with this dream once you attain it to make a meaningful impact on your life and the lives of others.

5. Maybe you cannot have it all, but you can have what's most important to you.

6. Remember that while the company can fire you tomorrow, your family won't—nor can you be fired from the community, the environment, or the world in which you live.

7. Compromise does not mean you have to compromise all the time; determine what you must have and make that the priority on which you will try not to compromise.

8. Being organized helps you avoid the extraneous and focus on the big picture.

9. There is always a reason to be at the office—only you know when it is critical and when it is not. Be discriminating.

10. Make it look easy even when it is not. That is a sign of power and of being in control of your destiny.

11. Sometimes, a special project really will require round-the-clock attention to the job—organizing a major customer conference, for example, or taking the company public. To do it right, you

will have to throw your life into imbalance. Don't let guilt reign, but when the project's done, redress the imbalance.

12. Can you integrate work and life in your present company? Maybe not. Think hard about transferring to a company that takes the concept of work/life balance seriously.

13. To set the example for work/life balance, start in your own organization. You might decree that there are to be no meetings and no late nights on Fridays, or perhaps you'll require that everyone take the full vacation allotted to them.

14. Nobody does it all—all the time. Not men or women, leaders or kings. Take time to prioritize what is most important.

15. Don't worry about things out of your control—control what you can and let the rest just happen—it will anyway.

STRATEGY 2

Corporate Life: Fit In or Move On

Bill: In all the coaching I do with executive women, one of the major struggles is for them to adapt to the upper echelons . . . to work on fitting in.

Janice: Women are great adaptors. We've been conditioned to adapt from an early age—to be nice, to be polite, to not fight. When we go to school, we continue that behavior by concentrating on getting good grades. And in business, we learn how to work hard, to dot all the i's and cross all the t's so that we get recognized. At that point, we feel we've arrived; we have adapted, we've played by the rules. Now you're telling us we have to adapt again at another level?

Bill: That's right. I find women in corporations dismiss the requirement to adapt at this level.

Janice: Perhaps we just don't see it. We don't realize we're now in a different ball game, the rules have changed and we have to adapt again. Perhaps the rarefied air clouds our thinking—and we get little feedback and few clues at this level.

Bill: Janice, no one offers advice once you make it to the big leagues—you are expected to know the rules.

Janice: But these are man-made rules.

Bill: The men who made the rules control the top for now. Play by *those* rules; then get the power and change them.

SCENARIO:

There were lots of vice presidents in the giant pharmaceuticals company—and Mary M. was one of them—but there were very few senior vice presidents. Promotion to SVP, in fact, was a clear signal that you had arrived, that you were part of what everyone called the "Top Team" that effectively ruled the organization. So when Mary was appointed to a senior vice president post, given the title, the new office, and all the associated perks, she knew she had made it—on her own terms and in the eyes of everyone else.

It had long been her goal. She had literally dreamed of becoming SVP. In the dream, she saw herself taking charge, visualized the changes she would make, fantasized her own success. She had clearly visualized her future as discussed in the first strategy. So the minute the promotion was announced, Mary knew exactly what to do.

Her aim was to set her personal stamp on "her" organization. She wanted to prove she was deserving, that she was "that good." Within days of her appointment, she had summoned all two hundred–plus staff who comprised her division to meet with her, unit by unit, bypassing her seven direct reports in the process. To all, she laid down the law—the rules and procedures that would prevail from now on, the goals she expected these people to achieve, and the date by which they had to be achieved. Period. Mary's dreams had been a rehearsal; now that she was onstage, she was letter-perfect, and she blitzed the division with absolute confidence and lightning speed.

Yet, she was almost terminated from the corporation. Six of her seven direct reports threatened to resign; a number of lower-level staff sought transfers. "Her" organization was in chaos and in an uproar. But because she was "that good" and such a star, the top team decided to give Mary a second chance and sent her for some serious professional coaching.

What happened? Simple. Mary hadn't read the signals about how life worked at the top of the corporation. She wasn't following the tracks the top team had laid out. *She* had made it—through hard work and by towing the line. Now that she had achieved this august level, surely she was home free to create her own organizational construct. Wasn't she?

Not even close. . . .

SURVIVAL OF THE FITTEST: ADAPT

The underlying theme is simple: You have to fit in, be accepted, and follow the lead of others before you can make changes.

In the physical world, where life is a constant competition for limited resources, adaptability means survival. The success stories of evolution are those members of a species that change to accommodate new environmental requirements. They escape unfavorable surroundings by jumping so high they can fly through the air, or they grow fur to confront an Ice Age, or they take on a camouflaging coloration that makes them invisible to the latest predator in the neighborhood. One way or another, they succeed where other members of the species fail; they often succeed at the expense of other members of the species. The characteristics these successful creatures develop through adaptation—the traits that keep them alive—are then passed down to their progeny via genetic code, and as long as the environment does not change again, the species is pretty secure.

The business world is equally Darwinian. In the competition for that limited resource we call power, those members of the species who develop superior traits through adaptation are the organisms who survive—and thrive—at the expense of others.

Men in the corporate world have been adapting to the environment for generations. They've learned to fly, grown the fur—not to mention thick skin—and figured out the right protective behavior for survival. Their success at adapting to corporate life seems to have been passed down as part of every male's genetic code; it's automatic, instinctive.

But women are still newcomers to the middle and upper reaches of corporate America. As a group, they haven't yet developed the selectively valuable behavioral patterns that bring advantage. What's more, women face something in their corporate environment that men do not—an entrenched dominant class defined solely by gender and constituting a virtual iron wall holding up the glass ceiling.

But here's the catch: Women can't remove the iron wall till they scale it. To do that, they'll have to adapt to the dominant class's culture. That's why adapting is the prelude and prerequisite to everything else in this book.

SCENARIO:

A senior-level human resources professional recalls being the sole woman at the company's succession planning meetings. It seemed "surreal" to hear only men's names mentioned as potential high-potential "corporate property." Joe, Bill, Robert, Paul: Everyone at the meeting knew them well, had played tennis with them, had lunch with them, had "run into them" on one assignment or another. When the occasional female name was mentioned—Andrea, Joan, Caroline—silence followed. The men at the meeting simply didn't know these women. After a pause, one of the men around the table would offer that "next year, maybe we'll get a better handle on Joan and maybe put her on the list." A seat at the table? It's hard enough to get your name heard at the table.

CULTURE SHOCK: SOFTEN THE LANDING

The dictionary defines an organization as "a structure through which individuals cooperate systematically to conduct business."[7] Of course, life in an organization isn't always entirely cooperative, and conduct isn't always all that systematic. Nevertheless, a common purpose joins the individuals in the organization; shared symbols and myths, common traditions and experience link them one to the other. The glue of that linkage is culture—the values and beliefs, the unspoken assumptions, the unwritten rules of behavior, the unconscious norms of thinking and acting that define "the way things get done around here."

We define culture as comprising four key components:

- The organization's type—what is its fundamental driver?
- Its leadership style—how is the organization run from the top?
- Its operating style—how do people interact in the organization?
- Its personality—what are the unwritten rules? What's the texture of the place?

It is all this to which women must learn to adapt better and faster than we have in the past, for all this is the culture of an organization. What makes this a demanding and time-consuming requirement is that culture can shift with various winds. Change of leadership, economic and political change, world events, and technological advances can all affect cultural climate.

What's more, there is not just one culture in a corporation but many—conceivably as many as there are subgroups in the organization. Some of those subgroup cultures are easy to spot; they're defined by function or staff unit or branch location. No one would ever confuse the culture of the finance guys and that of the marketing people . . . the culture of line managers and staffies . . . the head office culture and that of the people out in the field. Each is its own tribal caucus, clearly differentiated but perhaps difficult to define.

Cultures are also different at different levels of the hierarchy. At the bottom of the hierarchy, where the personnel ranks are both numerous and diverse, there can be numerous diverse cultures. That means there's more choice; you can shop around for the culture in which you're most comfortable, the values and behaviors in which you feel you fit. In the middle management ranks, corporate culture is to a great extent defined by performance; the symbols and customs of the corporate value system take second place to the bottom line. By the time you reach the upper echelons of corporate life, however, performance is a given, and the number of cultures has invariably shrunk to one—the one defined by the Chairman. There are relatively few of you at this elite level, so everything you do is noticed, and there is typ-

29

ically very little tolerance for deviation from the prescribed, accepted culture.

Yet it is at just this point that women almost habitually fall off the track. Time and time again, we have seen women of exceptional business sense and managerial talent simply come unstuck the moment they enter the rarefied ranks of senior management. Clearly, it isn't that they suddenly lose their talent or forget their skills. Instead, it is invariably that they fail to adapt to the clubby new culture that rules at the top.[8] Their evolutionary instinct tells them to keep on doing what they did to get to this point: stand out, achieve more than anybody else, get the A-plus, run the show *their* way. That instinct is unfortunately "a mistake," says Heidi Schneider, an EVP of the asset management firm Neuberger Berman. The mistake, Schneider goes on to say, is that "a lot of women . . . come in to situations to make changes. They think they're there to change the rules. They're not. Not yet." They are there because they were chosen to fit in. Only then, after being accepted in the club, can they maybe change some of the rules.

WHY ADAPT?

In fact, in the senior ranks, where everybody thinks of himself as elite, rule-changing behavior—standout behavior—is, for better or worse, a cultural anomaly. Many of our female coaching clients are high-level corporate women of outstanding potential who simply cannot or will not adapt to the environment of the hierarchical level toward which they have been working for decades. "The problem," says one such woman, astutely, "is that to get to this level in the first place, I had to change the rules—to make my own rules. Now you're telling me I have to play by the rules. It just doesn't make sense."

Maybe not, but it's the reality. Stand out to get to the top, but once you're there, fit in. That close to the chairman's office, you're highly visible anyway; everyone's visible at that level and everyone's supposed to be a star. What you don't want is to be visible as "not fitting in." As one of the women we interviewed for this book was told by her CEO: "All I care about is that all my Pavarotti's are singing the same tune at the same time."

The CEO is right. After all, he picked this team. Remain aloof from it, and it's a little like questioning the CEO's judgment—not a good thing to do. What's more, the CEO's group of Pavarottis is small; anyone who sings out of tune is likely to be noticed in ways you don't want to be noticed—with potentially disastrous results. Chairmen are no longer interested in managing those kinds of people problems. You're here; he picked you; he expects you to make it work.

So whether it makes sense or not, scaling or removing the iron wall and shattering the glass ceiling must start with adapting to the culture that has created both—with blending in and making people feel you're one of them, behaving according to the norms even if you feel different. Says psychologist and executive coach Dr. Marilyn Puder-York, whose experience on adapting came during her career as a manager at what was then Citibank: "First you have to become part of the machinery. You have to adapt to get the power. Once you've got the power, *then* you must have the courage to make changes. Until then, the norms of the culture in which women find themselves must become rules to live by."

ADAPTING IS A NATURAL PHENOMENON

Adapting to your corporate culture is not capitulation. It does not require that you act like a wimp. Nor does it mean selling your immortal soul, denying your heritage or your gender, or becoming someone you are not. We see adapting as wisdom in action—playing the game by the rules until you win regularly. Women who adapt become, in Puder-York's term, "part of the machinery" of the organization; they increasingly fuel the organization's engines, and the more they're at the controls, the more controls they'll be trusted with.

But. There's always a *but* and in this case, there are two—at least two environmental situations to which you should not adapt. One is a culture that allows or encourages behavior that is inappropriate, dishonorable, or of course illegal—anything from playing fast and loose with petty cash to sexual harassment or operational malfeasance. Typically, such a culture values expediency. Emphasis on the bottom line and the need to perform at all costs has the potential to spill over into bad management. And bad management in turn can all too easily spill over into actions with which no person of integrity should be associated. Integrity, as you don't have to be told, is something that cannot be retrieved once lost. Adapting to a situation that threatens integrity would be self-destructive in the extreme.

The second situation to which you should not adapt is a culture that simply is the antithesis of you. When you reach for the power in an organization, the organization had better be one to which you can feel committed; it should be led by someone with whose style and corporate values you can identify. If the culture goes against your style and values, the alienation gap may simply be too wide to be bridged. You won't be comfortable, your colleagues won't be comfortable, and no breakthrough to power will be possible in such circumstances—or even desirable. Find another organization with another culture, one in which you can be you.

Jewelle Bickford, a successful investment banker and Senior Managing Director with Rothschild, tells of an early career experience at a major financial services organization. Although she had achieved one of the highest scores ever registered when tested for a position in investment banking, she wasn't making it there. She asked one of the very astute managers at the bank why, and he gave her a piece of advice she has long remembered and often used with others: "Jewelle, you have the razor-sharp skills and talents needed in an investment banker; go to a company that will celebrate your uniqueness." She was in the right position, but with the wrong company. Today, she often looks back to that as a turning point in her career and a major contributor to her success.

SUBSTANTIALLY SUPERFICIAL
BUT COMFORTABLY SPEAKING

In the old, old days, if you went to work for IBM, you wore a white shirt and had your barber give you the right cut. Anything else was simply "un-IBM," and given that this was a company that actually had a songbook and insisted on morning calisthenics, not looking like you belonged was tantamount to not belonging.

Those days are gone, right? The idea that your clothes or hairstyle defines you is pretty silly. After all, you've been hired by a company, not recruited by an army with its own uniform, its orders of the day, and its clear enemies. Haven't you?

Unhappily, those days are not entirely gone. A reality check confirms that many of the military aspects of corporate life persist. Foolish as all this is, we feel we would be remiss if we did not point it out.

In a way, of course, fashion and taste are the outward evidence of a culture. They're superficial emblems of corporate culture, but they *can* be telling, and they *are* worth paying attention to. The point is: People *do* pay attention.

For example: The senior managers in your corporation wear dark suits—even on casual Fridays when vice presidents on down are dressed in khakis and polo shirts. Golf is the preferred game; the weekend's sports disasters and triumphs are discussed each Monday morning at the senior staff meeting. Like the Chairman, the senior managers to a man drive sport utility vehicles. Everyone carries a canvas bag in lieu of a formal briefcase.

Does this mean that if you carry a Gucci bag you'll give offense? Certainly not. But it may mean that if you've got a casual canvas slung over your shoulder you'll transmit a message of consensus that will make your colleagues around the table almost unconsciously feel comfortable with you. In short, adapting to the culture at the top is not a matter of aping superficial points of style, but doing so can be a very smart move. People feel most comfortable with people and things just like themselves.

SCENARIO:

Karen G. adored high fashion and jewelry of every kind—from the delicate bracelet of precious gems that was a gift from her husband to the chunky costume jewelry she picked up at flea markets on weekends. When she was promoted to a division head position, she was determined to promote her wardrobe as well—from utilitarian pantsuits to more sophisticated designs she could further dress up with some of her favorite baubles. So for her first-ever senior division heads' breakfast, Karen walked in wearing a casually elegant linen suit with a swing in the skirt and a loose, easy jacket. Her pavé diamond earrings and matching cocktail ring sparkled. On her wrist was a kitschy charm bracelet, and around her neck was her new funky glass choker. She was sure, she said, that she "looked like a million dollars," but in her own words, "I felt utterly naked; I have never been so uncomfortable in my life." None of her colleagues— seven men and two women—said a word; no one looked at her askance. But in a sea of gray suits and white shirts, Karen felt like a chorus member singing off-key—and doing it louder than anyone else. There was nothing wrong with what she was wearing—the designer suit and the pricey jewelry would have made a splash at a party on the weekend—but here, it just felt wrong. As one of only three women at her level, "I might have gotten away with it," Karen says. "I might have accustomed the men to my style of dressing. But I did not think this was a principle worth standing up for. Even more, I didn't think it was a principle worth standing *out* for. I wanted to be comfortable, and I wanted my colleagues to be comfortable with me." That afternoon, Karen ordered a half dozen simple suits in conservative colors and fabrics—her office clothes. She bought a pair of black pumps and a pair of beige pumps. And she reduced her daily jewelry diet to a pair of small pearl earrings and her wedding band. If this is a scary story, at least it has a happy ending: Within a year, Karen was promoted yet again.

Of course, it's a trade-off. Saving the fun clothes for home or weekends, as Karen G. quickly did, was not a great sacrifice. In fact, Karen found it a small price to pay for acceptance. It is precisely because what you wear, the sport you play, even the drink you like at the end of a day can all speak volumes; these superficial totems have substance. If you ignore them, do so knowingly.

SIX STEPS

But of course, what really counts in adapting to the culture is getting in tune with the way things work in the organization and, equally important, staying in tune as the environment changes. The break-through approach for doing so proceeds in six steps:

1. **Classify the organization.** What type is it? Some set of common attributes gives this organization its particular character. Go beneath the surface to type your organization.

2. **Read the leadership style.** What are the practices of the organization's leaders? What behaviors do they value and reward in people?

3. **Read the operating style.** How do people interact—and how do things get done?

4. **Read the personality.** What are the unwritten rules and group dynamics that give the organization its specific temperament and tendencies?

5. **Assess your fit with the corporate culture.** Is it a fit? Are you right for this organization? *Can* you adapt? Complete the critical self-assessment questionnaire coming up in step 5, pages 45–46, and find out.

6. **Develop and execute a plan.** Commit to make yourself a part of this organization's machinery, an individual valued by the leadership, someone who interacts successfully to get things done in the organization, someone whose personality is in tune with the organization's personality.

Obviously, this approach is an ongoing process as the organization changes—and as you change in adapting to its culture.

Step 1: Classify the Organization. Corporate culture has long been a subject of study and analysis. From William H. Whyte's 1950s classic, *The Organization Man,* to contemporary classics by such scholars as Peter Drucker, Rosabeth Moss Kantor, Tom Peters and Robert Waterman, John P. Kotter, Edgar H. Schein, and many others, corporations have been explored and explained, probed and profiled. It is not our intention to repeat what the experts have said—you're far better advised to go directly to their works. But we've drawn upon some of their time-tested theories in our description of the four classic organizational types—analytical, driven, traditional, and innovative. In fact, most organizations likely will exhibit traits of all four of these cultural types, but one type typically predominates.

In the *analytical* corporation, numbers and data rule. An issue isn't an issue until and unless it is measured. The style in the analytical corporation tends to be numbers-driven, heavy on reporting, tightly buttoned, formal; control is paramount.

The *driven* corporation—the get-it-done organization—moves at crash-and-burn speed to make the sale and move the goods. The perspective is always outward: What does the client want? What does the market say? The driven corporation aims for nimbleness—for turn-on-a-dime behavior, sometimes to the point of chaos or confusion; it is in perpetual motion taking the market's temperature and responding to its needs. "Move move move" is the mantra.

A process mentality commands the *traditional* corporation. It lives by the book: the book of systems management, of processes and procedures, of rules and regulations. The style is bureaucratic; the aim is to bring order out of chaos and to get it done through the organization's minions. There is an old-style, stately slow attitude in the traditional organization—almost a passivity. Even in the twenty-first century, compared to other organizations, this one is a lumbering giant; it moves—but slowly.

Creativity is the watchword at the *innovative* corporation, in which it will always "be better tomorrow." The innovative organization extols out-of-the-box thinking and prizes intellectuals in casual dress. It wants to nurture the generation of ideas. Today's Internet dot-coms are good examples of innovative, future-oriented organizations: Mere ideas aren't sufficient; they're out to shift paradigms. Anarchy is encouraged. Risk-taking is nurtured. Technology is a cornerstone. They are their own harshest critics. The aim is not just to sell a product or service but to revolutionize the way things work.

We've devised a matrix of the four classic organizational types and turned it into a worksheet—Figure 2.1—you can use to profile your own organizational type. Keep in mind that your organization, like all organizations, will undoubtedly exhibit traits of all four cultural types; what the worksheet will do is help you determine the dominant type—at least, as of this moment.

On the worksheet, note the behaviors within your organization that correspond to or reflect the style and attributes of a particular type. In the next column, rank the behaviors you've noted in order of their importance within the organization—not just their prevalence but their influence or power.

For example, your organization may be both structured and formal in attitude and feel but at the same time fast-acting, with a driven, get-it-done style. Think hard about which set of attributes is more crucial, more fundamental, more central to the soul of the orga-

Figure 2.1 Four Organizational Types.

Type	Style	Attributes	Dominant Behaviors	Order of Importance (1, low–4, high)
Analytical	Measure it	Analytical thinking, numbers-driven— control, structured, formal, reserved		
Driven	Sell it	Fast action: move move move—get it done, informal, casual, open, client-focused, confused, chaotic		
Traditional	Build it	Systems mentality, bureaucratic—processes and procedures, conservative, "old-style," slow—passive		
Innovative	Create it	Fast, casual, outside-the-box thinking, intellectual, risk-taking		

nization. On your perception and that of others, assess the behavior of the organization's leaders as a first clue to the type of organization. As you go through this exercise, you're likely to find that the process of examining your organization in this way is itself a valuable tool for understanding the culture in which you work and how you need to adapt.

Step 2. Read the Leadership Style.   As someone once said, "a corporation is not a democracy." It is a power hierarchy in which the direction is set at the top; that's where the big compensation packages are, that's where the smarts and experience supposedly reside, that's who speaks for the corporation—often, quite literally. One corporate CEO we know refers to managers of whom he approves as "horses"; those about whom he's not so sure are "mules." The two words have entered the corporate vocabulary and have filtered down through all levels of the organization.

Similarly, John Reed's bizarre locution "Net net net"—used as the prelude to a summary or conclusion—was a standard Citibank-ism for years even before he was the institution's Chairman.

At Microsoft, employees know that when Bill Gates says he has "a natural instinct for hunting down grim news," he means it. "If it's out there, I want to know about it," Gates proclaims. "The people who work for me have figured this out."

General Electric runs on "Welchisms," sayings and buzzwords of legendary CEO Jack Welch. "Sharing best practices" and "boundaryless behavior" determine how operating units interact with one another. Warned that the company's gargantuan Six Sigma program might allow bureaucracy to creep back in, Welch defined an attitude for everyone in the organization. "I don't give a damn about a little bureaucracy as long as we get the results. If it bothers you, yell at it. Kick it. Scream at it. Break it." And on the subject of long-term growth, Welch's remark that "You can't grow long-term if you can't eat short-term" flatly defined the culture of one of our era's most successful corporations.[9]

The fact that the buzzwords of the leadership become an integral part of the language in an organization is indicative of the power of leadership in defining style, environment, and all the elements of culture.

In a very basic sense, therefore, the leadership sets the tone for how the rest of the organization functions on a daily basis. Everything about the style of the leaders—the values they cherish, the things they do, even their personal quirks—quite literally determine who gets rewarded and why. That is why reading the leadership style is so essential to the achievement of power in both the short-run and the long-term.

The key is to determine how all those values, practices, and quirks translate into a *style* of leading. We see four classic leadership styles, four ways in which any organization is directed:

- by dictate
- by committee
- by consensus
- by delegation

Leadership by *dictate* is simple: The head honcho calls the shots, and everyone else falls into line. The dictate from the top is translated into the appropriate set of tactics and functions for each descending level of the hierarchy. Execution cascades downward like a stream tumbling down a multitiered waterfall.

In leadership by *committee,* an executive committee hashes out the overall strategic direction and sets the compass points. The committee thus shares responsibility for the organization's success or failure. Subsets of committees down the hierarchy reinterpret the overall direction and establish their own compass points.

Leadership by *consensus* mandates that agreement on a course of action be reached among independent, coequal professionals. The leader who is nominally in charge will typically bring to bear stacks of evidence for a point of view but will negotiate and deal until everyone is as committed to the point of view as he is.

Leadership by *delegation* pushes responsibility for tasks down to the lowest possible level in the organization. Trust and regular communication between boss and subordinate is required for employees to get the job done. People feel responsible and are held accountable for the tasks assigned.

As with cultural types, a single organization can exhibit a range of leadership styles. Perhaps the CEO leads by dictate, but your own group's chief prefers a consensus style. As long as each level of the hierarchy can meet the demands of the level to which it reports, a variety of styles can work.

Which leadership style fits your organization? Use Figure 2.2 to rate it on a scale of 1 to 5, with 1 low and 5 high, to determine the dominant type.

Figure 2.2 Four Classic Leadership Styles.

Leadership Style	Attributes	Your Organization
Dictate	Head honcho calls the shots	1 2 3 4 5
Committee	Executive committee and subsets share responsibility for success or failure	1 2 3 4 5
Consensus	Independent, coequal professionals agree on a course of action	1 2 3 4 5
Delegation	Each member of the team is assigned tasks, held responsible, and recognized for solving specific problems.	1 2 3 4 5

Step 3: Read the Operating Style. How do people interact in your organization—and throughout the ranks of the corporation? How do the people who work there make things happen?

An organization's operating style is its way of functioning. It's the way you and your coworkers execute the course of action set by the leadership. Think of these styles also as definitions of corporate "community"—that is, they describe how people work together in an organization.

We've identified four basic types of organizational style:

- open
- political
- silo
- family-collective

In an *open* organization, people network with one another, give and take quid pro quos, and cut through or across bureaucracies to get things done.

A *political* operating style is one in which people tend to watch over their own turf. They often bring hidden agendas to meetings, and they play to win—often regardless of the means.

The *silo* operating style defines an organization in which each unit is its own enclosed structure, there is little in the way of group activity, and individuals are left alone to do their work in their own way and on their own terms—without a lot of meetings, rules, or requirements to interfere. As a result, people tend to be focused on their own agendas and are consequently willing to act quickly and decisively on their own.

Finally, there's the *family collective*, a community confident that it possesses all the resources and information it needs, a community of people who identify with each other, are willing to challenge each other about goals and tactics, and feel confident about the work they do. It's "all for one and one for all" in the family-collective operating style; all share the blame when something goes wrong, and all share the glory when it goes right.

Rate the dominant operating style at your organization on a scale of 1 to 5, 1 the lowest to 5 the highest, using Figure 2.3.

Figure 2.3 Four Organizational Operating Styles.

Operating Style	Attributes	Your Organization
Open	Networking to cut through bureaucracy, no organizational boundaries, high degree of professionalism	1 2 3 4 5
Political	Turf protection, hidden agenda, playing to win regardless of others, highly competitive	1 2 3 4 5
Silo	Individuals and units focused on own agendas, unit lines not crossed, little interaction needed across departments	1 2 3 4 5
Family collective	People identify with each other, share resources, glory, pain— very collaborative	1 2 3 4 5

Step 4: Read the Personality. The higher you go in the organization, the more essential it is to be attuned to its personality. Unlike type, leadership style, and operating style, personality cannot be neatly categorized; it's as variegated in organizations as in humans. And as with humans, personality is what is distinctive about your organization. It is shaped by the collective qualities and traits that spell out the organization's character. Defining organizational personality, therefore, is about as elusive as defining obscenity; but what has been said about the latter is equally true of the former—that is, you may not be able to define it, but you know it when you see it.

You can find clues to an organization's personality in the unwritten rules, the temperament or "tone of voice" of the organization, the rituals that govern life. The unwritten rules include such things as whether meetings tend to start on time . . . how they work . . . whether first-name terms prevail up and down the hierarchy . . . the subjects that are and are not discussed around the water cooler. Is it a company-picnic kind of place or one that budgets for departmental Christmas parties, with the CEO making an appearance at each party, like a monarch on a royal progress? Is it the kind of organization in which people drop in on one another's offices, or does a more rigid, formal style rule?

What's the temperament of the organization? There are corporations whose ponderousness you can sense the moment you step off the elevator . . . others in which the air seems to crackle with excitement . . . still others that seem to embrace all who arrive. Organizations can be warm or cool, cheerful or solemn. It's not a comment on their effectiveness or on their appeal as places to work; it's just their tone of voice. They may seem to welcome you when you first arrive, but they are testing you. If you fail to read the personality signals early on, you may flunk the test.

The rituals that govern life in an organization include a lot of those points of personal style we discussed earlier—the superficial emblems of taste that, for better or worse, can speak volumes about an organization. In addition, rituals include all those procedures people in organizations follow whether they're written down in manuals or not—the kinds of procedures that define how you *really* get an extra credenza or a new printer for your office, which outside photographer to hire for the division dinner, whom to see in the budget office when you need more funds for your pet project. Are meetings collegial or a forum for evaluation? Always assume the latter.

Nebulous these organizational personality traits may be; elusive they certainly are. Still, there are some basic organizational personality types we're all familiar with. In Figure 2.4, see which ones you recognize, and identify the type—or types—that dominate in your organization.

Okay. You've charted your organization's type, identified its leadership style and operating style, and defined its personality. Now let's put it all together to draw an overall portrait of your organization.

Figure 2.4 Organizational Personality Types.

My organization is:

Gunslinger vs. Methodical—a shoot-from-the-hip personality that doesn't bother with precision

Butt-Kicking vs. Nurturing—a get-it-done personality impatient with what is happening to people either personally or professionally

Individualist vs. Collective (or Team)—a place where the self is most important and where people pursue tasks separate from others; team good is secondary

Short-Term vs. Long-Term—a today-focused personality not interested in sacrificing for a greater good tomorrow

Risk-Taking vs. Risk-Averse—where taking risks and even getting your hand slapped is better than not taking action to avoid the risk

Workaholic vs. Family Friendly—a place that values face time and being at the company at all hours and at all costs; family issues are not on the radar screen

Multipersonality vs. Uniform Personality—no one personality prevails, resulting in inconsistencies in policy and practices

Identify the dominant descriptor in each category on the following worksheet, Figure 2.5.

The descriptors you've circled should capture your organization's overall culture. It's a picture of what you'll need to adapt to. Be alert to it. If your values, operating style, and personality do not fit in, it will reject you.

Step 5: Assess Your Fit with the Corporate Culture. Now that you know what the culture is, can you adapt to it? Do you want to? Are you at home here? We assume, of course, that as a woman on the senior management track, you have already made a commitment to this organization. Nevertheless, organizations change. You change. Leadership changes. Maybe the organization to which you committed yourself has become an organization with which you identify less strongly. Or perhaps you were just hired in new to the senior level.

Steps 1 through 4 of this adaptation breakthrough approach have given you a snapshot of today's organization. Now, to assess if you and your organization's culture are a good fit, take the quiz that follows; it will help you determine the strength of your commitment to the culture.

Figure 2.5 Overall Organizational Assessment.

Type	Leadership Style	Operating Style	Personality
Analytical	Dictate	Open	Gunslinger vs. methodical
Driven	Committee	Political	Butt-kicking vs. nurturing
Traditional	Consensus	Silo	Individualist vs. collective
Innovative	Delegate	Family collective	Short-term vs. long-term Risk-taking vs. risk-averse Workaholic vs. family friendly Multipersonality vs. uniform personality

Mark each statement as either True or False for you:

1. I enjoy working with my peers in this organization. T/F

2. I believe the organization's values fit with mine. T/F

3. The way this organization operates on a daily basis suits my style. T/F

4. The organizational structure does not impede my ability to get things done. T/F

5. I believe that I can achieve my one-, three-, and five-year goals at this organization. T/F

6. I understand and can play by the rules of this organization. T/F

7. People in this organization work well together. T/F

8. I know of at least three people either on my level or senior to me whom I admire and can emulate without sacrificing my personal style. T/F

9. I have practiced the kinds of behaviors this organization prizes, and I believe my conduct was well received. T/F

10. I am comfortable practicing the behaviors this organization values. T/F

11. I believe instinctively that overall this organization is a good place for me. T/F

12. Compared to other organizations in which I've worked, I rate this organization higher. T/F

13. The organization offers a lot of freedom for me to decide how I want to work. T/F

14. Basically, people are judged on how well they perform here. T/F

15. If I make a mistake, I believe I will get support from my peers and my superiors. T/F

16. I believe I can trust people in this organization. T/F

17. The organization uses its resources efficiently and is, overall, an effective organization. T/F

18. The organization offers opportunities to learn new things. T/F

19. I am satisfied with the opportunity to make a difference in this organization. T/F

20. As one of the few senior-level women in the organization, I believe I have a shot at the top spot or the most senior-level position I seek. T/F

If you answered True to sixteen or more of these statements, you are at home in this organization. If you answered True between ten and fifteen times, you are close to home but perhaps not fully committed and comfortable. Look hard at the analyses of the culture to find the commitment gap; adapting here may be tough. If you answered True fewer than ten times, you should re-evaluate your place in the organization; adapting may ask too much of you. If you answered True less than five times, move on to another organization or another position—either in this company or another. Exiting is a way of adapting, too.

Step 6: Develop and Execute a Plan. Comfortable? Committed? If so, it's now time to make yourself a part of this organization's machinery. It's time to plan how you will adapt, how you will adjust your behavior in interactions up, down, and sideways throughout the organization. Two very effective guideposts for this adjustment are the organization's own role-model heroes and the articulated themes of the organization's mission or strategic goal.

First, watch the court favorites—that is, those who have the boss's ear and the boss's confidence. Check out their behaviors: How they operate, how they treat people, what their body language says. Which of their behaviors can you emulate—and which would make you uncomfortable? Fill in a worksheet like the one shown in Figure 2.6.

Moreover, figure out what it is these corporate heroes bring to the table that makes them so valuable. Do you have this? Can you get it? Can you do better?

Figure 2.6 Behavioral Analysis 1: The Court Favorites.

Names of Court Favorites	Their Operating Style/Behaviors	How They Treat Others	My Similar Behaviors

Second, consider what actions you can take to show you support the articulated themes and values of the organization, and fill in a worksheet like the one shown in Figure 2.7. If *teamwork* is an organizational watchword, for example, you might seek appointment to a cross-departmental task force so as to demonstrate your own comfort with teamwork. Once appointed, you will of course need to identify the culture of the task force itself—type, leadership style, operating style, personality—and then adjust your behavior to it.

Now it's time to plan how to emulate the behaviors pertinent to your organization's culture. An adaptation plan is like any other, except that you have complete control over performance; it is all personal performance—your own conduct, your own behavior.

Figure 2.8 is a sample adaptation plan; it asks you to plot where you interact with others, what you must do there, and when. The specifics listed under Forum/Interaction may be different for your situation, but the overall template should work whatever the specifics.

Figure 2.7 Behavioral Analysis 2: My Actions.

My Behaviors: note as (+) or (−)	What I need to do more of/What I need to change to support the culture or themes of my organization

Figure 2.8 Adaptation Plan.

Forum/Interaction	What I Must Do	Timetable
Meetings with the boss		
Meetings with executive group		
Dept/division meeting		
One-on-one meetings with peers		
Meetings with subordinates		
Task forces		
Informal get-togethers		
Company social events		
Companywide meetings		
Other		

SUMMARY

Fitting in is as much an art as a skill. You'll need a bit of both to succeed in becoming part of the organization. If you do, you can create an audience; then, when you have the organization's full attention, you can change the rules. Start by analyzing and understanding the type of culture you are in, its leadership style, its operating style, its personality. Go where your uniqueness will be celebrated. Assess honestly whether you really can and want to fit in, then execute a plan to become part of the machinery. Think as you like, but behave as others do. Blend in.

Commenting on the difficulties of adapting to an organizational culture, Marilyn Puder-York suggested picturing "an American male CEO going to Paris to head a French company. He doesn't know the language, the customs, or the company. Imagine how difficult it will be for him to feel accepted." Women entering the higher ranks of corporate management are also going to a foreign country, but readers of this book are no longer interested in finding themselves accidental tourists trying to gain acceptance far from home. They're tired of visitors' visas that can be revoked in an instant. It's time for permanent residency.

It is true enough, of course, in Puder-York's words, that "the environment won't yield. You can't adapt the environment to your message, and you are the one who early on must make the first impression a great one and solidify that thinking about you. Changing impressions and labels is sometimes an impossible task. The label just sticks; that's why you have to manage the fit very carefully. You must adapt the message to the environment—massage it so it can be heard and accepted. What it comes down to is you have to market your message."

The message is: Women want *in*. They are ready to enter the inner sanctum of corporate power and to use the power to effect cultural change. First, however, they must adapt to today's culture. Everything else flows from that.

Risk-Taking: Be on the Line

Janice: Line experience is still the single most dependable path to power in corporate life. Bill, do you agree?

Bill: I do indeed. However, because women have so long been stuck in staff roles, they still have trouble getting on that path. Their background and training, not to mention the expectations of many corporate men, reinforce the assumption that women simply don't belong on the line. An old military attitude!

Janice: Certainly that is changing as more and more women come into corporations with MBA degrees and with native confidence about their P&L abilities. But for mid-career women, line experience remains elusive. It also remains the excuse men use for not giving women top jobs.

Bill: One essential is for women to think bottom line—to seize any opportunity that gives them any kind of P&L responsibility and to be seen as a business partner.

Janice: I agree, and I would add that even women serving in staff positions should make sure they're seen as having a P&L role. Whatever their staff job is, they should make themselves indispensable in it.

Bill: Staff budgets do have major P&L impact, that's for sure. By the way, one major company has done away with the whole concept of staff and line roles. All roles have P&L responsibility.

It's no accident that the modern corporation has borrowed its organizational rationale from the military. Like an embattled army, today's business corporation is in a constant campaign to achieve victory. In this campaign, diverse functions must all be geared toward a single strategic objective. Numerous tactical initiatives must be planned and implemented. Resources must be deployed precisely and effectively. And it must all happen while the corporation is being targeted by adversaries who may be equally well equipped and managed—maybe better. For corporate management, the task is not only to take that hill—that is, to achieve a particular objective for sales, or for enhanced shareholder value, or for added revenue—but to take it under fire. This is particularly true in our new information age, as the rush to get to market increases.

That's why the work of both military and corporate human resources is divided between staff and line. In the safety of headquarters, highly trained, highly specialized staff functionaries undertake the vast jobs of planning, coordinating, and supervising operations. Out in the field, line officers command the troops and make it happen. Where staff thinks about support and logistics, resources and supply, the line thinks about winning the war. Line managers and line officers live and work on the front line of the battle. They are under constant threat of gunfire. Their orders are unambiguous. And there are no second chances for those who fail.

In what used to be called "this man's army," the front line was where soldiers proved their manhood and where officers won their stripes. Ambitious graduates of West Point and Annapolis don't yearn for desk jobs at the Pentagon but for a war where they can demonstrate the one thing that counts in battle: successfully managing the operation that takes the hill. Take this hill today, and you get the chance to take a bigger hill tomorrow. While the staff officers back at HQ will be highly valued and greatly appreciated, it's the guys who take the hills who are first to move up in rank and responsibility, in honor and glory, in power.

In the business corporation, the front line is any job that has responsibility for profit and loss. That's where corporate officers prove their legitimacy and earn their stripes. Meet that goal and you're obviously ready for bigger responsibility. Succeed there and your whole resume is irrevocably altered. "A proven track record of P&L experience," the resume now reads, and that tells any corporate leader all he needs to know.

NOT JUST MYSTIQUE

No wonder there's a mystique about "the line." Those who've served there believe it has imbued their lives with a special grace. They belong to an exclusive club, a community that only those who have shared the experience can truly understand. Until you've done it, the mystique says, until you've felt the pressure of being shot at by the marketplace and the competition, until you've thought on your feet and made decisions in the midst of the cross fire, you don't really belong in the organization's leadership.

If women are going to grab leadership in corporate America, it's essential to seek, embrace, and execute profit-and-loss responsibility on the front line of the organization.

Most of us could name important corporate leaders who made it despite having little or no line experience. Financial wizards, savvy lawyers, creative marketing geniuses have all made it to the top in various corporations, and it may be that your corporate culture has room for such deviations from the usual path to power. But in most corporations, P&L experience remains a tested, proven means not just of upward advancement but of entrée into the councils of leadership. And while blazing prodigies may make it to the top by other routes, this book is aimed not at the very few whose exceptional gifts light their way upward, but at the vast majority of corporate women who confront the iron wall of male power and privilege. Besides, the odds are good that if you're a *female* blazing prodigy, you're going to have a harder time than a man when it comes to stepping over or around P&L experience.

THE FEAR-OF-FAILURE TRAP

What's keeping women out of line jobs? As we hinted in our discussion at the top of this chapter, it's partly a matter of expectations. The old perception of the corporate woman—a person cheerfully suited to the pink-collar arena of PR or HR or marketing communications—is dying a slow, agonizing death. Even if women are no longer automatically assumed to be newsletter writers, they are seen as "belonging" in administrative support functions where their habits of organization and their clever ideas will serve them well. It took the United States Army a long time to see women in positions of command authority; it's taking corporate America even longer.

But women bear some of the responsibility as well. They've typically shown a reluctance to embrace P&L responsibility. While many have accepted the responsibility when it's been thrust upon them, the majority of women have shown little eagerness to actively go after line jobs. Why? What's behind the reluctance?

We've thought long and hard about this. Based on our collective five decades of corporate experience and on our discussions with the women interviewed for this book, we think it comes down to one simple factor: fear. Why? What, precisely, are women afraid of? Women may not like reading this word, but let us elaborate on what kind of fear we are referring to.

Are women insecure about being held accountable? We don't think so. In corporate life as in life in general, women tend to show a willingness to accept obligations and their consequences. In fact, they sometimes assume accountability for mistakes and failures with which they are only peripherally involved—if at all.

Are women overly cautious about going where few women have gone before? Hardly. You're reading this book precisely because you want membership in a club that's nearly exclusively male.

Are women simply more risk-averse than men? That is a standard assumption, and it has some validity. But what we think is really at the heart of the issue is that women are risk-averse in a different way.

While women are just as willing as men to take a calculated risk, they seem to work off a different calculus when it comes to balancing risk against opportunity. Women tend to see the downside more than the upside, but that's probably because they have more to lose. To a woman, the possibility of failing at a P&L job sounds like a career-ending failure. And given the obstacles women still face in corporate America, can anyone say for certain that that's not the case? For that reason, women tend to analyze all aspects of a possible line job much more rigorously than men would. They certainly analyze it more rigorously than they would an available staff position. Too rigorously, in fact. Disproportionately rigorously—until the line job itself looms as the possible be-all and end-all of their career. Then if women take the job and fail, they're pretty sure it's their fault.

Men, by contrast, probably don't even consider the possibility of failure before they take on P&L responsibility. It's just another step in the career. And if a man fails at a P&L job, he tends to see the failure as something that *just didn't work out,* something he'll just have to adjust to—hardly the end of his professional career.

For women, the fear of failure in a line position is a classic example of self-sabotage. It's a trap, at the bottom of which is one of those secrets men have been keeping to themselves for generations—namely, that line jobs just aren't that hard.

Janice remembers a one time human resources director remarking that his new line position was a piece of cake compared to his former HR job. In HR, he said he "worried about the entire corporation, with few lieutenants, whereas now I'm just responsible for one of five divisions and have a team of managers to support me and take responsibility."

OUT OF THE BUNKER, ONTO THE LINE

So unless you're a born CEO, one of those naturally gifted corporate leaders whose talents cannot possibly remain hidden for long whatever job you're doing, it's time for you to go after a position in which you will hold profit-and-loss responsibility. Proving yourself in a line position is probably the only sure-fire way to launch yourself on the path to power.

Will it require sacrifice? Probably. At the very least, expect disruption and inconvenience as you leave the safe, cozy bunker you now inhabit. It's a choice, after all: Do you want the power enough to make the sacrifice, or would you just as soon close this book and go to yet another meeting? You can't move ahead while you're sitting pretty. In the words of Johnson & Johnson's JoAnn Heffernan-Heisen: "You've got to step out of the comfort zone." Yes, the distinctions between line and staff roles are fading. Still, if you have a choice, go for the line slot or make your staff position accountable for a P&L.

SCENARIO:

Barbara W. was a respected vice president at a major consumer products corporation. In nearly two decades in corporate life, she had held only staff positions, working her way up the traditional pink-collar path. At age 43, despite an excellent record, she knew her lack of line experience clipped the wings of her upward progress. When a line job opened up in a small subsidiary 2300 miles away from the head office—and stayed open and untouched for seven months—Barbara decided to go after it. It entailed a range of sacrifices: a demotion in title, a cut in salary, an unwelcome relocation for herself and her family. She put all that aside and applied for the position.

Under the circumstances, Barbara's eagerness for a job nobody else wanted counted as sufficient qualification. She spent three years at the job, doing it well enough to keep the subsidiary contributing significantly to the corporation's overall bottom line. It prompted senior management to see her in an entirely new light, and when they summoned her home to the head office, she returned as a conquering hero. Today, she is a group vice president running three divisions—and clearly one of the corporation's superstars. The lesson? In Barbara's words: "Sometimes you have to take one step back to take two steps forward."

If that's a sacrifice, it's worth it. Only a line job can catapult you two steps forward on just one foot.

FIVE STEPS

Every woman interviewed for this book affirmed that managing P&L responsibility was a sine qua non of the corporate woman's power agenda. "Where women *have to* get to are the line jobs," said futurist and author Edie Weiner of Weiner, Edrich, Brown, Inc. "If you ever want to run a company," advised Bravo Networks President Kathy Dore, "it is important to be part of the line."

How do you get the line job and get started on this reliable path to power? Here's a five-step approach:

1. **Focus on line responsibility.** It's a question of mind-set: a way to think about yourself and your career in order to position yourself for seizing the right P&L opportunity.
2. **Get the skills and capabilities.** When the opportunity presents itself, you're going to have to be prepared. Start now.
3. **Broaden or create your opportunities.** Keep your nose to the ground inside and outside the corporation, and start sniffing

around for deals you yourself can bring in and turn to your own advantage.

4. **Broadcast your availability and desire.** You can't win by hiding in corporate closets. You've got to come out in the open to see and be seen.

5. **Think and act like a line manager.** Stuck in a staff job? Manage it like a line job. In a line job? Act like a leader.

Step 1: Focus on Line Responsibility. Getting your mind around the idea of P&L responsibility is the basic and critical first step. Accept the fact that line experience is necessary for you to get the power you want, change the way you calculate risk, assign yourself to going after a line job, and set a timetable. That's what women need to do to develop the mind-set appropriate for P&L responsibility.

The necessity of P&L experience may require you to move to Podunk or Kathmandu and take a salary cut. So what? If the opportunity is right, you will soon be able to have your pick of locations, and your compensation will climb. Don't spend time thinking about other routes to power or about being an exception to the rule. Put that thought and energy into the task at hand: getting the right line job and proving yourself in it.

And speaking of Kathmandu, do not underestimate the importance of getting international experience—even in a hardship post. Overseas assignments tend to the opportunity to play many different roles, be part of a lot of activities not necessarily germane to your area, and to interact with country heads who hold global responsibilities. And when you return to the home office, you'll have experience that sets you apart. Of course, distance can be a risk. The women we spoke to made it part of their agenda to keep closely tied to the doings back home when abroad, and to cultivate their network when back home. The risk, in short, may be worth taking.

Adopt a new calculus of opportunity versus risk. On the opportunity side, the new calculus reckons that seizing P&L opportunity can bring big-time success. On the risk side, the new calculus tells you that you can manage the downside, and that if you do happen to hit rock-bottom, you can pick yourself up and start all over again. In other words, failing doesn't mean you are a failure. It means you made a decision and tried to make a difference; it didn't work—and now it's time to move on.

Assign yourself the task of either getting a line job or elevating your staff job to the stature of a line position. Treat it as you would any assignment from the top tiers of management, as a strategic objective you can't afford to miss. Give yourself a time limit—a reasonable wait for the right line opportunity. When the time limit is up, if there's still no indication that management is willing to give you line responsibility or afford you the same power in a staff role, reconsider your situation in the corporation.

How long a time limit should you allow? Exemplifying the difference between male and female perspectives—and perhaps in attention span—Bill says one year, Janice says two. We have compromised by advising that you split the difference: Give yourself eighteen months max, and when the limit is up, reassess what has occurred and the probabilities awaiting you. Then decide whether you're willing to wait another year or not. In a chart like the one shown in Figure 3.1, identify the line positions you really want, determine why you want them, and assess the probability of attaining them. This will help you to focus on what is significant and possible.

Figure 3.1 Step 1: Focus on It.

Line Positions I Want	Why I Want Them	Possibility of Attaining Them (scale of 1 to 5)

Step 2: Get the Skills and Capabilities. Something has been keeping you from feeling confident about taking on P&L responsibility. What is it? What don't you know? What can't you do? Whatever it is, now's the time to get it. Or maybe you already have P&L responsibility and it's time to move onto bigger responsibility. What's holding you back?

Do you lack mastery over a particular subject matter or academic discipline? Go to school. Are you missing a particular skill? Take a workshop in which you can study the skill and practice it.

In our world, the Internet has become a wide-open portal to a world of learning in a universe of formats. It makes it possible to search out courses, workshops, seminars, books, training media, and more that teach you what you need to learn and that equip you with the capabilities and resources you need to possess. You no longer need to live near a university or business institute, nor is it necessary to attend a course in person. The Internet brings you basic learning and directs you to the right resources for learning more.

Is it a matter of keeping up? Maybe you've fallen behind in your knowledge of the latest information technology. Given the pace of change in IT, where "the latest" occurred an hour ago, just about everybody falls behind. Find and bookmark a technology news reference service on the Internet—there are scores of them—and log on every day.

Or maybe you're not sure of your people skills. Since you've only ever managed a staff of two assistants, you lack confidence about your ability to work through a number of lower hierarchical levels to motivate a larger team. Log on and search the topic to find that you can pretty much pick your time, place, and method of study from among scores of books, multimedia learning programs, hands-on workshops, lectures, and training seminars.

Bottom line: There's no excuse for not acquiring the skills and capabilities you'll need to do the line job well, comfortably, and confidently. Start now. Complete a chart like the one shown in Figure 3.2 to identify what development you need and how you will get it.

Figure 3.2 Step 2: Get the Skills and Capabilities You'll Need.

Line Position(s) I Most Want	Skills/Capabilities Required	Relevant Skills I Possess	What I Lack	Where/How to Get What I Need

Step 3: Broaden or Create Your Opportunities. You're the one going after that big line job, so it's up to you to keep your eyes open for an opportunity—or even better, to create the right opportunity. You're at a corporate function for your husband's company . . . or at a charity event . . . or at that workshop you're taking to hone your management skills. You're networking, meeting new people, renewing acquaintances with old colleagues. Wherever you are, whatever you're doing, you should be grazing the business pastures for that potential opportunity for your company, an opportunity to which you could contribute in a line position. You need to "recruit the deals" for yourself—especially those deals that can become P&L responsibilities for you.

At the same time, recruit potential deals within the organization as well. Perhaps there's no line slot available, but there is an opening as deputy to a line manager. Go after it. Once you've got it, make yourself a problem-solver and fixer, the natural successor to your boss or, alternatively, so indispensable that a new position is created for you.

Emphasize that your staff function exists to support the line. Demonstrate that support. Recruit the line managers who can benefit from using your staff function; make the benefits a reality, showing the line that you can function on their behalf and on their terms. The lesson you want the line to learn? You're a colleague, a peer, a natural for the next line position. Act like one. Show your value—the authority and self-confidence of the expert you are.

Get out of the bunker any way you can. Join task forces or committees dealing with bottom-line issues. Stretch your role. We know a vice president of HR who routinely goes along on sales calls. The aim? To become a colleague to the sales force and visible to customers at the same time. It's a far cry from the usual perception of the "HR staffie."

Step 4: Broadcast Your Availability and Desire. This is no time for ladylike modesty. Let people know you want to be a candidate for the next opening on the line—or for more responsibility, if you already have a line job. Senior management can't be expected to read your mind or guess your desires. Spell them out.

The best way to do that is to ask for the job. Don't necessarily wait for your next performance review, either. Get on the boss's calendar and announce that you would like P&L responsibility, that you intend to work toward that goal, and that you would like his support. Ask him what he thinks you need to do to get there—and ask as well what he and/or the corporation might do to invest in your getting there.

When you take a course or join a workshop, let your superiors know about it—and let them know why. When you have brought a deal into the company, make sure senior management knows who started the ball rolling. Advertise not just your achievements but your aims as well. Let the world know that you want P&L responsibility, you're preparing yourself for it, you're helping to create the opportunity, and you'll be ready for it when it comes.

Step 5: Think and Act Like a Line Manager. Line managers think and act in terms of profit and loss. While you're waiting for your turn as a line manager, translate that construct of thought into your current position. If you are in a staff role, you can directly impact bottom-line profit and loss by initiating ways to indirectly add to profits and stem or mitigate losses. Get your people to follow your lead, and soon your whole team will be partners in your ambition. Think and act like a line manager, and pretty soon people will start seeing you as one.

Let's suppose that en route to a line position, you are managing a marketing communications unit that is a cost center with no expectation of profit. Thinking and acting like a line manager, you can demonstrate that you can cut costs and raise productivity while maintaining—even enhancing—the quality of what the department delivers. How? Your market research has demonstrated that a new product feature would enhance sales. Or perhaps your market segmentation project has uncovered an emerging subcategory of the market that has yet to be tapped.

Or maybe you're in charge of an administrative function that serves solely in a support role as a boiler-room utility. You might translate the line manager's construct of thought to your function by creating a cascading system of performance benchmarks, so that measures of timeliness and accuracy are improved routinely and on an ongoing basis.

Find the way to treat your staff role like a line job. Adopt the vocabulary of the line. Adapt to its culture. Know the business from soup to nuts. Let the powers-that-be see that you're ready to move out of the safe bunker of headquarters into the battleground on the front line. Convince yourself that you're just the woman to take that hill.

ARE YOU READY FOR THE LINE?

Want to find out if you're ready for the line? Answer the following questions honestly.

1. Do you think constantly about the company's bottom line as a measure of your success?
2. Do you have the skills you need to take on a line job in your company? If not, can you get the needed skills in a two-year period?
3. Are there several line jobs in which you might be interested?
4. Do women hold at least 20 percent of line jobs in the organization?

5. Are you willing to take a lateral or downward line position in order to move up?

6. Are you able and willing to relocate into a line position if necessary?

7. Are you willing to take an international assignment to get a line job or broad staff position?

8. If you currently have a staff job, do you manage the function as a line person?

9. Are you viewed as a business partner by those who have P&L responsibilities?

10. Do you relish being accountable for profit targets?

If you answered "No" to three or more, you may have difficulty assuming a line position, so you should probably reassess your interest in pursuing line authority.

Senior Management: Lead and Feed the Boss

Bill: Men and women approach the boss quite differently.

Janice: Women have some old conditioning on this issue. Raised to please, we don't know how to get the boss comfortable with us. We want to be friendly and be liked, but we know there is a professionalism we want to maintain. Our younger colleagues seem to be less hung up about this balance of getting the professional respect and being liked personally. We want to know we have both.

Bill: There's the issue, right there. Women tend to look for feedback, approval, acceptance. Their instinct is to build the relationship on a personal basis, whereas men see the boss as "The Boss" in a more or less command-and-control way, not as someone you should ever get too personal with.

Janice: Women are often the only one of their sex at the table, so they revert to what comes naturally—trying to be liked.

Bill: Unfortunately, it's the wrong tactic. It's particularly damaging because a solid working relationship with the boss is a critical factor for corporate success.

Janice: Women who focus on what is relevant to their boss seem to keep the boss's attention and get a seat at their table. Women should do a variation of male bonding—get close to the boss without getting too close and without sacrificing their female side.

Bill: Not easy—a real balancing act! But worth doing, because the boss is crucial to a women's path to power.

In the movie of your career, your boss commands a starring role. You're the protagonist, of course, but the boss is central to the action, controlling the plot in just about every scene. Whether you're in an entry-level slot or just down the corridor from the chairman's office, the individual you report to is the one who mostly controls whether you'll move up, when, and in what direction. That makes him or her a dominant player in the drama.

That's why your relationship with the boss should be at the top of your agenda for gaining power. Your task? To ensure that the boss uses his power to advance you, to get you where you want to go. The way to do it is to bond with the boss, ally with him, cultivate a mutually nurturing and rewarding relationship—a mutually *useful* relationship. That is, make yourself useful to the boss—over and above doing the job well—and the boss will likely be more willing to make himself useful to you.

Heidi Schneider, EVP of asset management firm Neuberger Berman, was told by her very supportive father that she could be anything she wanted to be. And throughout her career not one, but four supportive male bosses reinforced this message. A savvy businesswoman, Heidi managed those relationships with care asking their advice and seeking to take on other responsibilities that were significant to them. While she aggressively and successfully built her business, she made the rules by playing by the rules and always focused on making her boss look good.

If you want to like your boss—or dislike him—as part of the bargain, that's a whole other issue; it is immaterial to the central role the boss plays in your professional life, the critical impact he can have on your career. Remember: At the top of the organization, no personal relationship ever replaces the need for performance.

EMOTIONALLY SPEAKING—DON'T!

And that's the part women typically have such trouble with. Depend on someone I dislike? Ally with an individual for whom I feel neither respect nor affection? Or—worse—seek personal advancement from someone I admire and like? That's not the way I was brought up, women tend to think, once again confusing a professional career in a business corporation with family life or friendship. Some corporate environments may indeed be familylike. Friendship—deep and abiding friendship—may indeed thrive in a corporation. But in the corporation, the bottom line is it.

Confusing the personal and the professional can have dire consequences, and corporate women seem particularly prone to such confusion. Men in business can hate each other's guts, get into horrific fights, and yet at the end of the day sit down and have a drink together. A woman will typically refuse the end-of-the-day drink on the principle that she doesn't *like* the individual. To the men, disliking someone is par for the course in the corporate world; of course you have a drink with the guy because *it's the right thing to do for both your careers.* To the woman, it's hypocrisy—hard to forgive, impossible to forget. Where men let the personal feeling yield to the professional requirement, women do just the opposite—they subordinate the professional need to the personal emotion.

A woman executive we counseled did go for the after-work drink following an extremely contentious day-long meeting. She started out tight-lipped and cold, still carrying the day's anger and letting everyone know it. By the second drink, she was right back in the fight, bitterly revisiting the same arguments she had lost earlier, arguments she should have left in the conference room. The upshot? Ostracism. Isolation. She had taken a social situation back into the conference room—where it did not belong. She was never invited out for another drink, but even more consequentially, she wasn't even welcome around the water cooler, wasn't included when folks gathered informally for coffee, wasn't really thought of anymore as part of the organization. Behaviors like this travel fast. Soon not only colleagues but also higher-ups see such women as nonteam players. It's a high price to pay for failing to see that the personal and the professional should be kept quite distinct.

SCENARIO:

Eleanor R., the highest-ranking woman in a Fortune 1000 corporation, suddenly found herself reporting to a peer when the chairman, looking to broaden the responsibilities of some of his direct reports, reorganized the company. Eleanor was furious with the decision and even tried to talk the chairman out of it. But the chairman could not have cared less that the re-org left him with no women direct reports—he had reduced the number of overall direct reports from seven to five; that was his concern. For Eleanor, however, the issue was what this might mean to her career. So she called the new boss to find out. Yet three days after the announcement of the re-org, he still hadn't called back. Colleagues advised her to "forget about it," saying that the new boss "doesn't do anything anyway." That just made Eleanor angrier: She could see herself working as hard if not harder and he would get all the credit.

She called her new boss several times, leaving a message each time. He in turn left two return voice mail messages assuring Eleanor that he would get back to her. She phoned again. And again. And again, finally leaving a cool and somewhat sarcastic message on the boss's voice mail. It "worked": He appeared in her office that very day after working hours. No sooner had he apologized, complaining about how busy he had been than Eleanor lashed out, hitting him right between the eyes. She saw his inattention as aloofness, saw the aloofness as indifference, took the indifference as a personal slap in the face. She accused him of insensitivity, claiming that he "had to know" the change had been "a real blow" to her. He had been a colleague with whom she had shared confidences; now he was her boss, yet she felt he was not nearly her professional equal.

Eleanor had entirely confused the personal and the professional—starting with her own emotions. She had allowed herself to become hurt, upset, and angry—the feelings of a victim. The place for her emotional venting was elsewhere, at home, with a friend—not at the office, and not in what should have been a professional exchange with the man who had power over her career. Even though she kept their conversation confidential, he didn't. Her so-called outburst with him became corporate legend. It damaged her career—permanently.

DO NOT DISMISS
THE DOUBLE STANDARD

When emotions dictate actions, control is lost and professionalism jeopardized. A cardinal rule: Never act or speak when you are angry. Men can follow that rule or not. For women the rule is a must.

Is there a bit of a double standard in that—in the finality of the impact of Eleanor's outburst on her career? You bet there is. In fact, double standards go with the territory here. A man who becomes angry is being assertive. A woman who becomes angry has lost control. The view will be negative toward the woman's display of emotion and not toward the man's. It's also the case, however, that, in general, men will walk away from their emotions or compartmentalize them out of the professional arena, while women not only engage their emotions more easily, they also more obviously wear them on the sleeves of their dress-for-success suits.

Do not dismiss these double standards. Men are used to the locker room and the antics that they shared growing up. Men didn't share those experiences with their mothers, sisters, wives, or daughters, and they are not going to share them with you. Janice recalls when her very special nephew, David, recounted the ripping abuse he took as part of being "trained" by his college football coach. What would have devastated her was just so much locker-room normalcy to David. Like most men, he was comfortable with the locker-room toughness and accustomed to "taking it."

In her book, *Play Like a Man, Win Like a Woman,* Gail Evans lists "Six Things Men Can Do at Work That Women Can't": They can cry. You can't. They can have sex. You can't. They can fidget. You can't. They can yell. You can't. They can have bad manners. You can't. They can be ugly. You can't." We would add a seventh: Men can be callous, insensitive, and too busy to be good managers. Women can't. Had Eleanor displayed toward a subordinate or peer the treatment she received from her boss, she would have been labeled cold, insensitive, and power-hungry. Her male boss was simply seen as a very busy guy who just couldn't get around to seeing her even four days after the re-org.

FIVE STEPS

Of course, it's important to remember that the boss is a human being, not a force of nature. He is not without emotions. He has an ego, frailties, baggage, problems, personality quirks. In fact, because the power he wields carries a burden of responsibility, and because such responsibility can be isolating, he may have more quirks, problems, baggage, frailties, and ego than the rest of us. In fact, there's an interesting thesis, advanced by Alan Downs in his *Beyond the Looking Glass* that narcissism is rife among corporate executives.[10] Watch out for those personality traits; they can trip you up. But they can also offer insights that will guide you to the right kind of bonding with the boss.

It's also important not to be sidetracked by all the supporting roles your boss may assume: advocate or nemesis . . . feedback person or constant critic . . . political advisor, coach, confidante, ally, partner, chum, sworn enemy . . . any or all of the above—and more. These supporting roles make a significant difference in the quality of your working life; indeed, you need to read the messages each contains. While his supporting roles are not necessarily germane to your power agenda, the boss's starring role *is* germane, and that is what you need to keep in mind first, last, and always. Look to him as simply the single most powerful instrument in your working life: the lever you can wield to propel yourself forward—or conversely, the immovable stumbling block on your path to power.

And how do you wield a lever, in Archimedes' phrase, to "move the earth"? Achieving high standards of excellence in your work only kicks up some dust. If you're going to create a bond that makes a difference to your career, you must make a difference to the boss's career. Whether he chose you, inherited you, or had you thrust upon him, you need to make yourself useful in a way that adds value to his success. That value-adding usefulness is, for both of you, a path to power. It's your leverage with the boss, your key to power.

The breakthrough approach for you, therefore, is proactively to determine what the boss needs for his success—and then to supply it. What will enhance his current strength? What weapon does his arsenal lack? Skill, technique, knowledge, ability, connection, linkage, contact—whatever is missing from the boss's reservoir is what you should be looking to provide. Everyone has an Achilles' heel—even the person at the very top.

So the first step is correctly to identify what the boss needs. To do that, look at him as both person and professional, as man and as corporate man, as human being and as a player in a particular environment.

The reason for this dual perspective should be obvious: Both the personal and the professional are brought to bear in the boss's relationship with you and attitude toward you. You cannot separate the great and powerful senior manager from the values he learned at his mother's knee or from the personal style encoded in his genetic make-up, or from the likes and dislikes gained over a lifetime and embedded into his thinking. Nor can you understand the person without knowing something about the professional experiences that buoyed him and burned him—the war stories that tell you what he values in colleagues, what bothers him, what pains him, what he'd just as soon not do. After all, maybe it's something you could do *for* him.

Step 1: What Makes the Boss Tick? To bond successfully, you'll need to read the person inside the boss's skin. Who is the boss? Corporate staff are quick to give the boss a nickname and treat him accordingly—with fear, emulation, deference, awe, disdain—yet rarely do they actually study the boss. Instead, they react to him without looking at what makes him tick and without considering what kind of person this is who has so much power over their lives.

So step 1 in your senior management strategy is to figure out what makes the boss tick and what kind of person he is. You don't have to be a behavioral scientist or a psychiatrist. You need only raise your antennae and read the signals. The signs and portents are everywhere.

We all have hot and cold buttons. Push the former and we respond with passion—maybe with anger, maybe with an embrace. Push the latter, and we turn off at once. Hot and cold buttons can be a minefield when you're trying to influence the boss unless you know precisely where each of them is and unless you understand the personality behind them.

For example, the CEO of a well-known advertising firm is a stickler for grammar who particularly hates the misuse, as he sees it, of the word *presently*. Lesson one with such a boss is never to misuse the word *presently*—in fact, try not to use it at all. Lesson two—perhaps even more important—is that you're dealing with a fastidious, rather pedantic personality with little tolerance for nuance, and you're up against a black-and-white outlook that is comfortable with absolutes and uncomfortable with anything that deviates from the absolute. Both lessons should guide your bonding behavior.

Examine the boss's temperament; you will want to respond to it at least, and you want to match it at best in meeting the boss on his own ground and making yourself indispensable to him. An aloof or welcoming temperament is evident even in the briefest initial contact. A few days of working together lets you know that your boss is the easygoing, walk-around type or a guy who prefers to stay closeted and out of the fray. One meeting provides evidence of gregariousness or its absence, informing you quickly that your boss is a social animal or a shy guy who is ill at ease on the networking circuit.

Of course, temperament is a sometime thing. Moods change, and chances are good your boss doesn't wear a mood ring that will clue you to his current state of mind. What *will* clue you to the boss's mood of the moment is "the grapevine," the tom-toms of the corporate jungle beating out the message that the boss is in a foul humor, don't go near him if you can avoid it, keep the bad news at bay by all means, hide in your office if you can. Listen well to those drums. Timing is everything and there is a time not to bring up bad news.

It's important to read the boss early—early in the day and early in the week. Monday morning may not be the best time to bring up heavy issues, especially if he had a rotten golf game over the weekend and is still grouchy about it. Sometimes, Monday morning sets the tone for the week. Alternatively, he might recover quickly from a bummed-out Monday and show up bright-eyed and bushy-tailed on Tuesday morning, ready to take on the world and everything in it. On a day when you're scheduled to meet with the boss on some heavy issues, call colleagues you trust and can joke with to see if they know that the boss is a happy camper that day—or if there was a morning disaster that blackened his mood. Delivering even good news to a boss in a foul mood can end up being a lost "win."

What's his comfort level? Whatever it is, you want to make sure he feels it around you. If he's the kind of boss who drops into people's offices, sits down, and puts his feet up on the desk, you want to get to a point where he does that in *your* office, where the chair next to your desk is the favorite one for the boss to kick back in. If his comfort level is formal, structured, follow his style, but try to find the triggers that render him less formal. Maybe he has a favorite author, or perhaps he's an old movie buff. Find your landing spots and develop comfort with him in the subjects that warm his personality.

Julie Johnson, an executive coach and President of the Reid Group, recalls asking a CEO client what he wanted Julie to work on with the woman VP she had been hired to coach. "Teach her how to chat," said the CEO. He complained that each time she came to his direct report staff meeting, she would go right into a business discussion mode. By contrast, he liked to get everyone relaxed by making small talk. The VP simply couldn't. Her failure was in not reading the boss's style—and therefore not delivering what he wanted. It's not good for the career.

What you're trying to find out is: Who *is* this guy? What's his background? Where did he grow up? Did he come from wealth? Work his way through college? Always want to run a company? Does he have sisters? A wife? Women friends? What are his values? Likes? Dislikes?

Walk into the boss's office. The walls and surfaces covered with photographs of his children at every stage of their existence from infancy to college graduation are a good indication that he makes time for his family and takes pride in them. The orderly desk, the neat stack of file folders, the line-up of books on the credenza are indications that this boss has facts at the ready; he is in command of his environment. Conversation lets you know whether he is conservative or liberal, even if politics are never overtly discussed. The heroes he cites are a hint that he prefers tradition to breaking the mold. He's proud of the fact that people in his division arrive early, stay late, and exhibit regular working habits, yet he also prizes bursts of creativity.

It all paints a picture of a complex human being, just as all human beings are complex. The reason you study this human in particular, however, is because of what he can do for you—and what he might do *to* you. Demonstrate your own analytical bent, your penchant for beginning with facts and your ability to master them. Stay away from politics altogether if yours oppose his, but if you're on the same side, support his views. Focus on what's tried and true in your own work and in your corporate behavior. Demonstrate your work ethic at all times—and your creative juices whenever you can. You are crafting a relationship that is going to advance your career. Knowing how the boss reacts when the hot and cold buttons are pushed will help you craft it right and forge a tighter bond.

Step 2: What's the Boss's Management Style? To make real contact with the boss, it's necessary to understand him as a professional—as a player in the organization—and to connect with him on those terms. You'll need to understand how he leads, how he works, how he interacts and communicates with others, how he is perceived. That understanding will set the parameters within which you'll forge your own individual connection with the boss.

Think back to Strategy 2 and determine the boss's leadership style. Does he lead by dictate, consensus, committee, delegation? What kind of manager is he—an analytical thinker who needs time to deliberate or a shoot-from-the-hip *doer* who likes to let a hundred flowers bloom and is willing to see some of them wither and die? Does technology drive him? Does he keep one eye on the markets at all times? What's his central theme?

Read the way your boss handles meetings; it offers tremendous insight into how you can get through to him. One highly successful EVP we know is nicknamed "the quartermaster" and works exclusively off what is reverently called "the agenda." The boss sets the agenda, lists the topics and speakers in a particular order, states a time limit for the discussion, and sets down the deliverable he wants to achieve on each agenda item. It's a methodology that's rigid, immutable, efficient, and from the boss's viewpoint, highly effective. It also offers insight into this boss's comfort level and hints at options for how to proceed—perhaps by supporting the boss through detailed note-taking, maybe by emulating the style in your own meetings, or perhaps by countering the rigidity and getting the boss to lighten up in private.

Then there's the managing director who invariably starts every meeting late and monopolizes the entire session with rambling out-loud thinking. Everyone agrees the meetings are inefficient bull sessions; people always say they could better spend the time working. Should you inject some of the quartermaster's style into this managing director's leadership palette? Can you offer clarity and rationalization that will complement the boss's rough-hewn style? (Be careful when you do!)

Is your boss the grown-up version of the most popular boy in your high school class? There are bosses who set out to be loved by as many people as possible—and who want it known that they are loved by as many people as possible. Can you help extend this boss's popularity?

Maybe he's the political type—mindful of his turf, continually reaching out to build coalitions and craft alliances that will protect and/or enlarge his power base. Like any politician, he'll need canvassers, advisors, ambassadors, strategists, even a press secretary. Become what he needs.

Or perhaps your boss is our Pavarotti pal from Strategy 2—the kind of boss who wants everyone warbling the same song on the same note at the same time. It won't be enough to sing along; you'll have to supply the sheet music or sound the pitchpipe or maybe hand the boss the baton if you're going to make yourself indispensable and step up to empower yourself.

How does your boss communicate? If you're to bond with him, you have to speak his language, communicate in kind. If he's the kind who jokes around for ten minutes before he feels comfortable getting to the point, plunging in impatiently simply won't work. If he's a no-nonsense guy, the latest light bulb joke or gee-whiz comments about last night's ball game will only convince him that you're the wrong person in the wrong place. Or is he the type who wants you to lead with the headline of numbers before going into the body text of whys and wherefores? Some bosses want the details, while others want to see the end product.

"During monthly business performance reviews, my boss would routinely ask me if my business was ever going to reach $XX million," says Jewelle Bickford, today Senior Managing Director at Rothschild. "I kept thinking that he didn't fully understand my business. So I would again take him through my business plan. And he kept coming back with the same question. Finally, I got it. I realized that all he wanted was to know 'when' we would be a $XX million business. I stopped taking him through the plan and simply said, 'Yes, by mid-year we will exceed our target.' And he was happy. Of course he understood my business, and he didn't need to hear me show how on top of it I was. He didn't want the details; that's what he was leaving to me."

Bottom line? It's a question of reading the boss's management style.

Watch your boss in action one-on-one with others. How does he treat and how is he treated by subordinates and superiors? How does he operate with customers? A style of interaction is evident in these exchanges. Observing and understanding the style will guide your own interaction with the boss—and matching his communication and leadership style is critical. For example, if you see him impatient with a colleague who is narrating a tale, that's a hint to you to get quickly to the bottom line. If he savors sharp one-liners or the pithy quote, search them out, have them ready, spring one when the moment is right. If the boss enjoys small talk before getting down to business, cultivate the art of small talk. If he laughs at his own jokes, laugh along. If he's formal, respect his respect for tradition.

Your boss has probably fired people in the past or reorganized them out of his line of sight. Find out who they were and why they're gone. Knowing the boss's definition of failure will tell you how to avoid your own failure.

Your boss has confidantes. Maybe he travels with an entourage of trusted aides. Who are these confidantes? Why does he seek out these particular people? You'll learn what the boss feels insecure about and/or what he values in people by getting to know the ones he hangs out with—or at least those he invites in for a chat, those whose offices he frequents, the people with whom he has lunch. These people make him feel comfortable. Figure out why. Observe how.

Your boss has an image—a persona—around the corporation and perhaps out in the wider world. The way he is perceived did not happen by accident; it tells you something about the boss's experience and style as an organizational player.

Complete your understanding of your boss as a professional by assessing his own potential as corporate property. If you've ever done a stint in marketing, you probably used the SWOT analysis: strengths, weaknesses, opportunities, threats. It's a good tool for analyzing your boss: what he's good at, where he can improve, what opportunities await him, who or what threatens his advancement. In bonding with your boss, you'll want to support him in what he's good at, fill in where he can improve, help him seize opportunities and avoid, elude, or beat out those forces that threaten his advancement. Understanding how he operates as a boss will help you do that, so fill out a worksheet like the one shown in Figure 4.1 to profile your boss.

Figure 4.1 The Boss's Behavioral Profile: SWOT Analysis.

The Boss's Strengths	The Boss's Weaknesses	Opportunities the Boss Seeks	Threats the Boss Confronts

Step 3: What Does the Boss Need (Whether He Knows It or Not)? Now that you know him as person and professional, it's time to figure out what's missing from the boss's arsenal. What does he need that he doesn't have? Or what should he have that can be important to him even if he doesn't know it—that he could use to his advantage if only he were aware of its existence?

In some cases, it's simply a matter of plugging a hole. The boss is a strong marketer but not as facile with the footnotes of the financials? Learn the numbers—every scruple of every iota of the numbers, every nuance and shade of their meaning. He's a brilliant analyst and strategic planner but has no head for sales? Become sales-savvy and you increase your chance of being the person he will turn to for sales expertise and sales ideas. Conversely, maybe he's a natural salesman but lacks the analytical tools that support his instinctive genius. Get those tools and become his chief analyst. Round out the boss's capabilities and you become indispensable to him. Provide him with a skill that he lacks but values—or perhaps one he simply does not enjoy doing—and you make him look better.

Often, however, more is required than simply one-for-one skills matching. Perhaps your boss has no talent for public relations; he's short on personality and less than articulate in public. It's a potential disaster the higher he moves in the corporation. (Yes, there are CEOs who lack this public relations ability, but it's an increasingly untenable position for corporate leaders in the twenty-first century.) You might seek to become the boss's personal PR consultant or even spokesperson—the silver-tongued orator who can speak for the boss—or you might advise him on speaking, or provide him with script and talking points, or persuade him to take a course in public communicating. There are many ways to supply a need. But approach the suggestion box carefully. Bosses typically like to hear how well they are doing, not where they need improvement.

Or suppose your brilliantly analytical and strategic boss with no sales talent runs a division that has nothing to sell. From years in marketing and sales, you've acquired the expertise your boss lacks, but you have no place to put it. Create a place. Launch a branding initiative for the boss's division and sell him on it. Bring your skills to bear to raise the division's visibility within the organization and advance its goals in a way that brings your boss new exposure—and makes you more indispensable than ever.

WHEN THE BOSS IS A WOMAN

Is any of this different if your boss is a woman? No and yes.

No because the strategy remains valid and the principles are the same. You still need to bond with the boss, and you still need to analyze who she is as a person, the kind of boss she is, and what she needs that you can provide.

Yes because there is an added dimension to being a woman boss, and that added dimension must become an essential part of your analysis. The added dimension? Like men, women at the top have their own idiosyncrasies. But because a woman is so often alone at the top, the way your boss got there will be an important component of who she is—as both woman and leader. Consider:

1. Maybe your boss is the *up-the-hard-way* kind. We all know her when we see her: She's the pioneer who fought the woman's fight all on her own, paid her dues, took all the guff the old boy network threw her way, and still came up a winner. Now that she's made it, she sees no reason why every other woman shouldn't find it as tough as she did, work as hard as she did, suffer as much as she did. The upshot? She tends to be harder on the women who report to her than on the men. She'll test you more rigorously and grade you more stringently. And, because she jealously guards the position she has attained—even if justifiably—she may be secretly hoping you'll fail. You'll need to find a way to help her shine while keeping your head below the firing line. Winning her over requires a careful analysis of who she is,

her career experiences, some of the war stories about her, and her history at the company.

2. Then there's the *boss-by-tenure*. She probably started out as file clerk to an unknown assistant vice president. As he rose through the ranks, she rose with him. Now that he's chairman, she is secretary to the board of directors, palace guard, appointments secretary, queen bee, and keeper of the seal. In fact, her list of significant titles and functions confirm that she still has the boss's ear. In her eyes, longevity confers distinction. Knowledge of the corporation and loyalty to it—although yours will never equal hers—are essential. The organization is her mother, the chairman is her son. Be good to both.

3. You certainly recognize the *superstar*. Her skills and intelligence are so glittering you can spot them a mile off. They outshine the skills and intelligence of most men in the organization—indeed, of most people. No one can match her; no one can compete. She's in a class by herself. It's a location from which it's difficult to see the problems, ambitions, or even the good work of others. Since you can't measure up on skills, you'll need to find another way. Look for what she'd "rather not" do, and do it.

4. Finally, there's the *favorite daughter*. She broke through to power with help. She was recognized, mentored, supported. Someone gave her a hand, and she understands the importance of extending a hand to others. She's a political creature and finds political skill a positive quality. She sees the need for nurturing and knows the value of constructive criticism. Seek both from her.

For both of us, it was illuminating if not overly surprising to find that almost all the women interviewed for this book preferred a male to a female boss. It wasn't surprising because the scarcity of women in power and the regularity with which they're perceived as "female bosses" first and foremost make them still anomalies in an organization. (It's also the sad fact that women tend not to find other women supportive—see the Epilogue.) If you're trying to break through to power, the straightest route is not through an anomaly but through the locus of power—namely, the male leadership. Our finding was illuminating for the same reason: At the start of the twenty-first century, women still aren't sufficiently at home at the top of corporate America. Women want to work for a boss who is comfortable being a boss—and who may be able to help them take the next step up the corporate ladder.

Step 4: Fill the Need.   Man or woman, what does the boss need? What do you need in order to supply the boss with what he or she needs? How will you get it? Do you need to take a course, make a new contact, refine a skill, create a concept? Once you've obtained what you need, how will you supply it to the boss? Write it down. Make a plan. Figure 4.2 will help you figure out what you need to do.

SCENARIO:

Maureen was chief of staff but yearned for a line job. She knew her boss valued and depended on her. Their relationship was close, almost fraternal. They shared secrets. She was certain he knew how much it would mean to her to have the line job. She routinely mentioned it to him—usually after a long day of meetings, when the two of them were winding up what Maureen called "the checklist," her list of issues that needed his input or his resolution. She would snap shut the notebook, lean forward, and begin. "You promised me a line job transfer," she would say, "and there's a

Figure 4.2   What the Boss Needs.

Behaviors of the Boss	What's Needed/Wanted	How You Can Supply It	Timetable

good slot over in the Consumer Products Division that I know I can do well in. Will you do this for me?"

"Maureen," he would inevitably answer, "this isn't the time" or "I can't spare you now" or "I've got to get home . . . ." He did not hear her; he simply wasn't listening.

She finally understood she had to change gears, take her career out of the realm of the personal and put it on a professional footing. She began to take a close look at her boss—not at the pal of shared secrets but at the organizational player she reported to. She found that what was most characteristic of him as both a person and a professional was his strength as a strategic thinker. That's what drove him; it was the key to his own success. If she was going to get through to him, she decided, it would have to be by appealing to that strength.

Maureen asked for a morning meeting with him. She brought with her a matrix that showed her skills and accomplishments. Another matrix showed the role she could play in the corporation—how she could make a contribution, how that contribution would redound to his own credit. She laid out a four-step action plan he could undertake to move her into a line slot while he covered his own flank with a strong chief-of-staff replacement.

He bought it. She was in the line job a month later. A year later, she was promoted to a level equal with that of the boss who had helped put her there. She had given him what he needed—in his case, a sound strategic reason to place a valued colleague in a highly sensitive position in the organization.

Step 5: Avoid Pitfalls. There's more to bonding with the boss than supplying what he needs. He's also a human being who wants pretty much the same things we all want: support, respect, to be liked, to be admired as a leader, to protect his staff, to succeed, to help you succeed, to blame you when things go wrong, to keep you in this job you're doing so well, to see you rise to the top—but at least one step behind him. In bonding with your boss, you must respond to what he wants as well as what he needs.

Sometimes, a boss just wants a little stroking. It *is* lonely at the top. Someone who shows up with something nice to say can look pretty indispensable. Be a conduit of good news you just couldn't wait to tell him. Of course, there are ways to stroke the boss and ways not to stroke the boss. The line isn't always clear, but use compliments cautiously and sparingly. There's a difference between complimenting somebody and acting in an overly ingratiating manner. One is pleasant, the other smacks of sucking up.

SCENARIO:

Michelle was a senior consultant bucking for principal at a prestigious consulting firm. One of the many ways the firm fostered creativity was to hold regular, all-hands meetings in the schoolroomlike auditorium. At those meetings, Michelle invariably sat in the front row and made it a point to praise the boss publicly and flatteringly. In a meeting with at least 400 people, many of whom offered important contributions to the discussion, Michelle's inevitable contribution was to register her admiration for the boss. "Paul's point is brilliant," she would tell the other 399 people in the room, "and I think we should implement his plan immediately."

Paul hated it. He gritted his teeth through the praise, wondering if he was blushing in front of 400 people. Eventually he drew Michelle aside and asked her to please cool her ardor; he even requested that she sit in the back of the auditorium for all-hands meetings. He felt awful about it because her admiration of him was genuine; it was the expression of it that made him uncomfortable. To him, it smacked of "sucking up," and it embarrassed him profoundly. It made him far less willing to think of Michelle as a principal, someone who would interact with clients at the highest level, someone who might continue this kind of behavior in those interactions, not to mention in the principals' conferences held every day!

Michelle got the point. But she never again felt at home in the firm, and she left shortly thereafter. While her talents were missed, her overt sucking up was not.

We'd like to be able to report that any kind of sucking up—genuine or calculated—makes any boss uncomfortable. But it simply isn't true. In reality, a lot of people—and perhaps a lot of men in particular—thrive on flattery, even servility. They enjoy being paid court to, and they respond to it. So while we don't encourage sucking up as a way to bond with the boss, we're surprised at how well it can work in some cases. And we would be remiss if we didn't say so. Again: Read your boss. If it works, use it.

What bosses don't want to hear is whining, negative news, complaints, or problems. At their level, they haven't time for any of that. If you're walking in with a problem, be sure you have the solution. If you're there to deliver bad news, bring a plan for change. If you've come on your own behalf, remember that this is a business and that you are in a business meeting. Bosses do not like the monkey on *their* back.

What should you never do? Never sell the boss out. Never complain about him to others. People just see you as a tattletale, label you as a complainer, and wonder why you tolerate what you say you can't stand. Besides, you'd better believe that anything you say can and usually will get back to the boss.

Exercise conversational caution; watch what you talk about. The old taboos—politics, religion, and sex—are good guidelines. But it's also a sound idea to avoid discussing corporate politics; what you say to your boss today might come back to bite you tomorrow. After all, he won't be your boss forever, but someone else will; and if it's the someone you've heard or said something bad about, you could find yourself painted into a corner with your own brush.

SCENARIO:

Val was as smart as they come, brilliantly educated, with advanced degrees in both business and operations research. Her pronouncements about people who were "not intelligent," in her phrase, were therefore likely to be taken seriously. But when she began to go on at some length about her own boss being "not intelligent" and about "management in general" being "not intelligent," the disdain became her signature. "This management team has risen through politics," she insisted to her peers; "they're not intelligent enough to run this place well."

When one of her peers was named chairman, however, one of his first acts was to fire Val. For all her education and brilliance, he knew that he would never be able to trust her; maybe she found him intelligent enough, but he was not about to take a chance. Her bad-mouthing could be poison, so he simply supplied the antidote before the bite: He got rid of her.

Never try to outsmart or outmaneuver your boss. Showing how smart you are in public by showing his weakness is a betrayal. He may be secure enough to let it go, but others will make note of it—negative note.

Lower your ego. It's tactically inept, as Maureen learned in seeking her line job, to chide a boss for not keeping a promise. It's equally

Figure 4.3 Lead and Feed the Boss: Dos and Don'ts.

Do . . .	Don't . . .
Be professional at all times	Put business on the personal level
Recognize that the double standard is alive and well	Speak or act when angry
Observe when your boss is in a good mood and act on it	Compete with your boss—support him instead
Model your boss's communication and management style	Badger your boss on what you believe is right—just inform him
Observe what your boss wants to get out of meetings	Be the bearer of bad news—unless you also bring advice, a solution, or a plan
Carry out those tasks your boss values	Whine or complain to your boss—instead, be a positive agent of change
Make your boss comfortable with you	Sell out the boss or tell stories about him
Supply your boss with what he needs, skillwise, to run the business	Out-ego your boss in front of others
Follow the boss's lead	Neglect or forget former bosses
Always make your boss look good	Overreact to a new boss being appointed in a reorganization

inept to ask him to do something for you *personally*. It isn't that he wouldn't do something for you; it isn't that he doesn't owe you. It's simply that me-based supplication is the wrong way to get what you came for. When you ask the boss to respond to your needs, make sure that what you're asking is good for the company as well as good for you.

And never forget the boss. You've been promoted? You've transferred? Gone off to career development training and come home to a new slot? Don't forget the guy who helped get you here. Keep the connection. Meet him for breakfast. Send him a note to congratulate him on his son's graduation, his daughter's new baby, his own professional moves. People like to be remembered. Besides, the former boss is part of the network, and the network, as we'll emphasize in a later chapter, is an essential path to power. Besides, who knows where the former boss might end up? Today's show of appreciation could pay you back with interest one day down the line.

Politics: Chat with the Boys and Get Elected

Bill: Corporate politics is something women seem to shun, yet they need to realize it exists and use it to their advantage.

Janice: Men seem to know from boyhood the raw effect of political as well as physical power. They seem to absorb and exude the knowledge naturally. Women, on the other hand, are conditioned to be coquettish to get what they want. That should be just one arrow in their quiver. Politics in today's corporation is alive and well. Women have to gain power by being politically savvy and playing to win.

Bill: Unfortunately, some women rely on being cute—and it gets some of them far.

Janice: In the end, though, women who win for the long-term and have staying power in the senior ranks will be those who know how to create a political power base and wield it.

"**M**an is by nature a political animal," wrote Aristotle in the fourth century B.C. So is woman, but until the latter part of the twentieth century, American women were conditioned to deny, dismiss, even disdain that part of their nature. One result: In far too many corporate women today, political incompetence is proving to be a formidable stumbling block to the organizational power they seek.

Political savvy is important not just in the corporation but everywhere, because politics is a fact of life. Maybe the ascetic holy man begging his rice along Himalayan byways is free from political influence and political dealings—but don't count on it. Otherwise, whether you're a shoe salesman or university professor, a bus conductor or a business executive, whenever and wherever people deal with people, politics is a reality—at its best, a fun, challenging, and beneficial reality.

In the corporation, it's a particularly pertinent reality. Corporate America is really a lumbering giant that moves slowly and operates with flawed management systems. Power is the way things get done in corporations, and corporations attract people who are eager to attain power and are comfortable exercising it. All those powerful people and powerful-people-wannabes want to further their individual agendas— to get *their* programs, *their* products, *their* plans, *their* strategies implemented. But in any organization, no matter how big or complex, resources are necessarily limited. There simply isn't room to implement every power-seeker's agenda. Nor is there enough power to go around; not every would-be mover and shaker will achieve the measure of power he seeks or thinks he deserves.

The result is competition—the competition that is the corporation's most powerful force for getting things done. Rivalry. Dueling agendas. Struggles for influence. Long-distance plotting and head-to-head sprints as the powerful people in the corporation compete against one another to advance their individual ambitions. That's where having a power base is critical.

Nobody except the chairman's nephew ever made it to the top of the power heap in corporate America solely on talent, charm, hard work, good deeds, and being nice. And not even the chairman's nephew can keep his power for very long without the support of others throughout the organization, preferably in key positions around the organization—peers, subordinates, and board members, plus outsiders with clout.

That's what a power base is: People around the organization and externally—preferably key people strategically placed—who can be counted on to help power-seekers achieve their individual agenda and ensure their upward progress.

EMERGE FROM THE BACK ROOM

Unfortunately, women in corporations typically fail to go after corporate political support strategically, when they go after it at all.

Look to history for the origin of the problem. In electoral politics, women have only recently begun to emerge from the backroom role to which they were more or less confined after winning the vote in 1920. Traditionally, it was men who were candidates, power brokers, and policy wonks, while women stuffed envelopes, passed out leaflets, and made the coffee. In the latter part of the twentieth century, however, women began hitting the hustings in great numbers, demonstrating to any who might have doubted it that women have as healthy an appetite for power as men and just as healthy an ability to glad-hand among voters and do deals among the political leadership.

But if women continue to make their mark in electoral politics, they have been far more passive about corporate politics. For one thing, corporate politics, as opposed to electoral politics, depends not on the quantity of your support—the numbers of votes—but on the quality of your support—that is, the influence and clout wielded by those who support you. It requires a level of strategic thinking and tactical targeting that has simply not been part of women's traditional skills conditioning.

After all, the kind of bridges women are traditionally good at building are personal bridges. Women excel at forming relationships born of person-to-person need and mutual affection. They're good at nurturing and mentoring but are not good at striking alliances with targeted individuals in order to advance their self-interest.

The bottom line? Putting it bluntly, many women waste a lot of time trying to help a lot of people rather than looking strategically to those people in and outside the organization who can do them the most good. And let's face it: Women have also been conditioned to disdain politics as something too rugged for their white-glove ways, too sleazy for ladylike consideration, too masculine to bother with.

That is the corporate woman's failure, and it's time she puts it behind her, emerges from the political back room, and begins to build a power base in the corporate political arena.

FOUR STEPS

It's important to distinguish the concept of a power base from that of a fan club. We'll get to the latter in Strategy 7, where we discuss how to brand your uniqueness and find people who'll love you for it. The people in your power base, by contrast, don't have to love you, although they will probably like you. However, they do simply have to support you.

We use the phrase "power base" interchangeably with what others might call a network, mentors, or alliances. You want to fill it with champions—advocates—not necessarily just pals. And you're looking for these advocates among a select group: powerful people both within and outside the organization.

Internally, you want as champions the people who influence decisions and can leverage resources. That includes your peers. Precisely because they do compete with you for those rare resources of people, time, and money, they're an essential part of the context in which you're seen to act. By forethought or unconsciously, through a casual comment or a prepared speech, peers can make or break you. Manage your relationship with them to make them champions, and you'll do yourself a lot of good.

Externally, you want as champions individuals who can influence your career at your current company or pave the way for advancement elsewhere. When you've finished finding and winning these internal and external champions, you should have a power base that stretches into every corner of the organization, that represents all the kinds of power the organization contains, and that has spheres of influence externally which will help you in your company.

Let's begin by creating a champions list. It will consist of people in positions of power with a plan for what you need to do to enhance or solidify their support of you. Start with your inner circle, then work outward from there. In Figure 5.1 we have listed some possible champions, but you will have others that may be more relevant to your career.

Step 1: Mapping the Power. Unfortunately, the human resources department doesn't issue org charts that show you the different kinds of power in the organization: who's got power (today), what kind of power, and how the holders of power are connected, or allied, or networked, or interlocked together for their mutual benefit. You have to create that particular chart yourself. We call it "mapping the power."

Start with a checklist of the kinds of power that exist by definition within an organization. There are two basic kinds: formal and informal power. *Formal* power is conferred by the organization. For starters, it's the power that comes with holding a superior hierarchical position. Certainly, the CEO, the CFO, and increasingly the CIO in today's corporations are powerful simply by dint of their title and the resources their position puts under their command.

In addition to the power of position, formal power is also conferred through the ability to hand out rewards. The people who hold reward power may be the actual dispensers of the goodies or perhaps just the gatekeepers guarding the goodies. Either way, they have the ability to provide something of value, and they are perceived as being able to provide something of value. The inherent power of the human resources function in most organizations, for example, is its capacity

Figure 5.1 Champions List.

Champions	In What Forum or Meeting I Can Make Contact with Them	What I Need to Win Them Over
(1) Internal		
Board of directors		
Superiors		
Peers		
Subordinates		
People in other departments		
Others		
(2) External		
Clients		
Professional associations		
Friends		
Clubs		
Neighbors		
Boards		
Political organizations		
Vendors		
Consultants		
School colleagues		
Professionals		
Others		

for influencing compensation and career, even though HR lacks the final decision-making authority on these issues. They are the advisors, persuaders, influencers of these decisions affecting your career.

Finally, formal power is conferred through the capacity to punish or strong-arm. The people with this kind of power are the muscle guys within the organization. They have the wherewithal to stop you from implementing your pet program . . . or perhaps they can force you to take on a project you don't need . . . or maybe they can insist that you or your people attend a training and development program . . . or maybe they require certain reports that seem controlling and onerous. Departments like Auditing and Accounting have this type of power.

The distribution center is an example of a place that can use its functional power to intimidate. Ever had the feeling your mail was being slowed down for no good reason except that the folks down in distribution were flexing their biceps just to let you know they have power? Matrix reporting relationships, too, also tend to be susceptible to such bullying. At a higher level, the office of the CFO is a prime example of formal power. The reports the CFO requires give the CFO's office inordinate power—especially if your organization is run by the numbers.

Informal power, by contrast, is not conferred by the organization but is earned—primarily through expertise, trust, the sheer power of personality, or sometimes by anointment conferred by a formal power holder.

If marketing is driving the organization, then the marketing genius whose every idea is a winner is powerful simply because of what he knows and can do that no one else knows or can do; the organization commits itself to giving him full authority to keep him coming up with ideas because the organization values marketing expertise.

The manager who makes you feel a sense of identification with his purpose, vision, and goals is powerful through the trust he inspires. Trust is admittedly a fragile thing, easily destroyed. But as long as it is maintained, the one who inspires it earns the power it provides.

Court favorites have power because they have the leader's ear. Whether they use that special access or not, they are perceived to have power—and so they do. At one organization we know, the head of human resources is treated like the son the chairman never had, and everyone knows that everything this HR head hears goes straight to the chairman. The watchword around the company is to "watch out for HR." No one trusts the HR head, but they pay homage to him.

Finally, we all know the individual in the organization who is just famous for being famous. He speaks, and people listen. Everything he says is assumed to be worthwhile. Everything he does is perceived to be a success. He has star quality—the power of image, of sheer celebrity. You can't analyze or explain it, but you feel it. It's real.

Keep a checklist like the one in Figure 5.2 handy as you map the power in your organization. Look for the people who fit the checklist's definition among your superiors, your peers, your subordinates,

Figure 5.2 Checklist: Who Has the Corporate Power—
A Guide to Mapping the Power in Your Organization.

	Type of Power	Attributes	Who Has It? Title
FORMAL POWER	Hierarchical	Title, position, resources (budget, people, geography)	
	Reward/Punish	Can stop or give go-ahead on projects or plans; has the approval/veto power	
	Muscle/Strong Arm	Can make onerous requests; or impede your productivity	
	Influence	Is part of the decision-making process; an influencer or advisor to the ultimate decision-maker; can help make or break an action	
INFORMAL POWER	Expert	Has expertise that is uniquely needed by the company	
	Trust	Inspires others, is sought out for constructive feedback, a balanced individual; has reputation as credible	

and others who do not report to you. Not everyone who is senior to you is necessarily powerful, whereas among those junior to you, there may well be possessors of considerable informal power.

How do you start looking? Begin where the action is.

Who was promoted recently—and who sponsored the promotion? Whose new project was initiated? What do people say about others in the organization? What's the talk in the halls, in the bathrooms, and over lunch? (Yes, you have to do lunch to hear what is being said.) Has the corporation made any recent acquisitions, decreed any new strategies, entered new markets, implemented new systems? If so, find out who wielded what influence on those decisions—that is, whose recommendations were listened to, and whose were not listened to. You might start your search by looking back through prior press releases and organizational announcements.

Remember that you are looking to build a power base, not to sign up a single "rabbi" to mentor your career and advocate for you. One is not enough. Things change: An executive or manager who is powerful today may not be so powerful tomorrow. Besides, your power base should include all the kinds of power on our checklist. While HR, for example, may not always be privy to the closed-door board-level discussions on corporate strategy, its influence power is, as the checklist reminds us, substantial. By the same token, that Gen Xer over in IT has no title, no muscle, and certainly no charisma, but he's so knowledgeable about e-commerce and the next generation of Internet use that his importance can't be underestimated. If you can, sign him up for your power base.

SCENARIO:

Ruth L. was politically astute enough to target one of the corporation's senior executives and major powerhouses to be her "rabbi." She believed that hitching her star to Jim's wagon would take her all the way to the corporate perch she wanted and felt she deserved. She cultivated Jim, helped him out, did his bidding—including some of his dirty work. In turn, Jim advised her, directed her, strategized with her about how she could influence others in the organization. He became her mentor, father figure, and protector.

So when Jim was suddenly fired in a palace coup on a Friday afternoon, Ruth was completely vulnerable. She had lost her sole source of protection and her only link to the top. With her loyalty to the new team in question, she herself left the organization two months later. The moral? When you map the power in your corporation, don't just target one individual.

Step 2: Win 'Em Over, Sign 'Em Up. The formula for winning political support and building your power base relies on an impelling motivation that is fundamental to all human beings: self-interest. "What's in it for me?" may be the basic question of human interaction. A satisfactory or persuasive answer may be the most effective instrument for getting things done.

Some people think *self-interest* is a dirty word. That's naive. Self-interest doesn't equate to selfishness; it's not necessarily a cousin to greed; it certainly isn't a synonym for corruption—although certainly, all those unpleasant attributes can spring from and/or serve self-interest. But assuming that self-interest is somehow impure gives a bad name to the rewards we all seek when we go to work—financial compensation for work done, recognition, excitement, fulfillment, some sort of legacy. The personal agenda is as real as the professional agenda; in most cases, in fact, the two are symbiotic.

Within your corporate organization, you will win people's support by persuading them that your self-interest is intimately bound up with theirs, or that their self-interest is dependent on yours, or that your self-interests are in some way mutual and are better served when they and you are strategically allied. Answering people's needs and wants is a good way to create a strong following. Best of all is when you can persuade the people you target for your power base that you have the wherewithal to help advance both their professional and personal agendas—and that you're ready, willing, even eager to do so. Give people credit. Compliment them publicly. Let others know you value their work. And in return? It is understood that some day, they'll do the same for you.

This is the way the world works. In legislative politics, they call it horse-trading for votes to get bills passed. In global politics, they call it writing treaties and establishing alliances. Corporate politics is no different. To build a power base, target people who can help you advance, provide them something they need or want, and take a figurative IOU in return.

For the Gen Xer over in IT, providing something he needs or wants may consist simply in easing his way into corporate life; perhaps helping to smooth some of his geeklike rough edges, show him the ropes, take him along to a meeting where he can interact with some senior people. The quid pro quo? He understands that you may be calling on him from time to time, that you'd appreciate hearing from him about new e-commerce initiatives, that you'd just like to keep in touch—maybe pick his brain now and again.

For the HR head who sits on the committee that marks you as "corporate property" or "dispensable," the contract and quid pro quo may be more complex. Perhaps there's a project the HR head wants to see implemented, one with his name on it, and he's not finding the support needed or the enthusiasm he'd like. Perhaps you're in a position to deliver that support and enthusiasm—where it counts. Your quid pro quo? You've begun to realize that the know-how in the brains of the Gen Xers from IT could be a big help in advancing your marketing plan and getting it funded. You'd like HR to look into transferring one of them out of IT into your department, maybe find a nice slot and create a job description with a pretty title—e-commerce officer—and attractive benefits.

In fact, that's a nice deal, because in cashing in your IOU from the HR head, you're delivering a new favor to the Gen Xer in IT, and setting him up for a quid pro quo to be delivered later.

To put the power base building formula into action, therefore, your first step is to find the thing your targeted powerful person wants or needs. What project is he or she pushing? What initiative is the person trying to get off the ground? Or, equally compelling, what problem is the individual facing? Who or what is in the way of the individual's forward or upward progress?

Once you've taken the measure of the project or problem, determine how your area of the business or you personally can help—what value your department can deliver, how your offering can help execute the individual's business plan, or how you can mitigate or eliminate the obstacles to the individual's advancement.

In other words, what do you have, what can you do, what's in your power that persuasively answers the individual's what's-in-it-for-me question? Find it and provide it, and you've put one more building block into your power base.

The form in Figure 5.3 is a checklist for figuring out how.

Step 3: Your Campaign Agenda. Did you ever see a politician on vacation? There's no such thing. At a resort, on the beach, in the mountains, touring the downtown of a world capital, politicians are always looking for votes. They *want* to be recognized, approached, talked to—not so much because it pumps up their egos, although it may, but mostly because they can't afford not to be in the public eye and in touch with public concerns. After all, even if they just got elected, they're always running for office. That's their business.

It's your business, too. No matter what it says in your job description, you're always running for the next office, and that means that

Figure 5.3 Mapping the Power: Winning Them Over.

Who Has What Kind of Power? Who What	The Power Holder's Agenda, Project, or "Need"	What I Can Do to Earn an IOU from the Power Holder

you're always looking for votes. The power base you build from among the powerful people in your organization is your starting point, and you need to be cognizant that every day there are forums, meetings, or encounters at which you must build this internal constituency. The chart in Figure 5.4, Campaign Trail Targets, will help you focus on how to maximize your opportunities with these people. But the organization's influencers and leveragers are not your only constituency.

There are influencers and leveragers outside the organization as well. You should get to know them, make yourself one of them, demonstrate that you belong in the power arena and are comfortable there.

Join an appropriate professional association. Become part of your community's business circle. Attend executive forums. Volunteer to work on a charitable event; next year, volunteer to run it. Sometimes, you can actually buy a ticket to the power club.

Take a course or attend a conference—both to reinvent yourself and to meet colleagues. If the organization won't pay your way, pay for it yourself—and let the organization know you've done so. You will have both honed your skill base and widened your network to include people from other companies who do the same job or need the same skill.

Keep in touch with those people. You can share ideas and think through problems together. And knowing what's going on in another company also is a means of keeping tabs on the opportunities that may open up there. Today with email, there is no excuse not to widen your network and stay connected.

Clients should be your allies as well. Regardless of the area you run or the business you are in, you have clients who are external to the organization. Human resources and marketing professionals deal with a lot of external vendors and consultants who may be very powerful by their contacts. Don't mistreat or dismiss the clout of the individuals who serve you—they too can be part of your power base. Where you have external clients, be sure to give them more than the product and services your company provides. Develop those relationships and build a group of powerful clients who become your "raving fans."

Business travel is a great way to extend your range of contacts and line up prospects for your extended power base. The person in the next seat on the plane, the only other woman in the business class lounge at the airport, the guy you share a taxi with to the center of town—any or all of these can become useful nodes on your network, whatever their current positions or areas of responsibility. After all, politicians kiss a lot of babies and shake a lot of hands. Consider the campaign trail targets who are most important to you and using Figure 5.4, outline how you can win their vote!

Figure 5.4 Campaign Trail Targets.

Internal Campaign	What Is the Specific Event/Situation?	What I Can Do to Win Votes
Task forces		
Committees		
Business social events (client dinners, etc.)		
Senior management meetings		
Special events		
Other		
External Campaign		
Clients		
Professional associations		
Country clubs		
Other clubs		
Charities		
Not-for-profit boards		
Seminars/Workshops, Speaking engagements		
Other		

Step 4: Keep Track—and Keep Tracking. One brick doesn't make a foundation, and one favor given and retrieved doesn't make a power base. Building your power base is an ongoing task. You'll have to continually take the temperature of your organization's politics, continually identify the movers and shakers both inside and outside the corporation, continually look for opportunities to make yourself valuable to them.

It's a little like driving a car. Your eyes are on the road ahead, but you also glance into the rearview mirror, checking the side view mirrors, turning your head to make sure nothing's in your blind spot. You're concentrating on your own track and your own forward motion, but you're aware at every moment of what's ahead, who's coming up fast behind you, the dangers and opportunities on all sides.

Same with corporate politics. Look around you. Everyone has an agenda, and everyone could use help with their agenda. You have an agenda, too. It's to advance to the highest power inside and outside the organization. Start laying the groundwork now so that when the time comes, your power base will be there to give you a hand as you step up to the power you seek.

POLITICAL SAVVY

Finally, it just takes some savvy. For role models, watch the men. They play the game as if born to it. Carol Tabor, former EVP for Lang Communications, put it this way: "Men know how to look the boss straight in the eye and agree that the sky is blue when it's about to pour."

And a successful senior investment banker talked about her four years at one of the top five banks as the worst experience of her life. "I hated it because it was 90 percent politics and 10 percent business. I never saw so many incompetent people making so much money for so many bad business decisions. I told my boss what he wanted to hear without being two-faced. He appreciated it, but he was the exception at the bank. It was a real learning opportunity. After years of experience and some scars, I've gotten better at how I phrase things."

It is time to drop the baggage and stop being victims of the political world in which you operate. Men don't take their marbles and go home when they lose a round; they understand it's part of the game—no big deal. Women must learn that lesson as well.

Here are some tips on how to be politically savvy:

1. With superiors, peers, and subordinates, reach out to find the common ground; then meet them on that common ground and get to know them.

2. Give others credit, but make sure they know and see you give them credit.

3. Information is power—especially when the subject is corporate politics. Get the information by letting others talk. Then keep the information private by holding it close to the vest: no "he said, she said."

4. Help a peer find and execute a solution that achieves the peer's goal, then suggest the peer help you spread the solution around the organization—under both your names.

5. Build a reputation as a compromiser, not as someone "out to get" people.

6. Stay above the fray; Never be heard bad-mouthing anyone; talk business, not personalities.

7. Be sure you are seen as approachable, and not holier than thou.

8. Make your subordinates your champions: Get them thinking positively about what they do, and they will "market" both the department and you.

9. Ask veterans and superiors for their advice. The highest form of flattery is to be looked upon as an expert and asked for help. The person asked will be grateful—and will be impressed by your intelligence. Besides, veterans and superiors do have wisdom to impart; make use of it.

10. Make people feel good—all the people you come in contact with. Make them feel important. If they go away feeling "high," they'll remember you for it.

11. Always strive for champions who will tout your excellence. There's no such thing as a true meritocracy in corporate life.

12. Pick your issues and don't get hung up on winning and playing to win all the time. Choose your battles and then let your colleagues win. Pyrrhic victories are deadly.

13. Don't take a bad day personally; leave hurt feelings at home and focus on the task. Learn from it and move on.

14. Show enthusiasm and a positive attitude, never negativity or emotion.

15. Keep private matters private. Be known as a trusted confidante.

16. Forget the notion that "it isn't enough to win; others must lose." You don't win by beating up a peer: What goes around really does come around.

17. Be a subtle suck-up. Pick your key issues; other times, agree with the boss.

18. Remember the company is not your family—vent at home not at work.

19. Trusting others to keep a confidence is foolhardy. Like the telephone game, what comes back to you will not be recognizable.

20. You can't control what people say about you, but you can control what they know.

21. Treat your colleagues well—make allies even of your rivals.

Communications: Be Business-Wise and Business-Brief

Bill: The stereotype that persists inside the corporation is that women talk too much—and say too little. Too much detail, too much analysis, too much dancing around the point.

Janice: However, the research shows that men actually talk more than women at meetings. The problem is that women spend too much time teeing up before they hit their points. They are not direct.

Bill: Because of this, men often tune out women physically and mentally. One woman I coached actually noticed men leaning across the conference table to block her physically. It's an apt metaphor: Men block women's communication in the centers of power—literally as well as figuratively.

Janice: Maybe women should follow suit. If women are not heard, they will not get to the top, much less succeed.

That we're born knowing how to communicate is as much a myth as the statement that women in corporate life talk too much. Bill called this latter the "stereotype that persists inside the corporation"—and it persists despite significant evidence to the contrary. A

Wall Street Journal report found that men actually talk more than women in meetings and conferences,[11] just as little boys raise their hands and speak out more than little girls do in school. In fact, one reason that men's ideas are accepted more readily and more often than women's ideas is precisely that men talk more. It's the shotgun idea: Spread enough ideas around, and, like random buckshot, something will hit a target.

Women don't speak *enough* in corporations. More to the point, they are not heard enough when they speak. The reason for that is the same simple reason that women are not sufficiently well represented in the boardrooms or at the helms of American corporations: They're women, they're not yet quite seen as belonging. In many cases, in fact, they're not yet quite seen or heard at all.

YOU DON'T NEED PERMISSION
TO SPEAK

Janet Green, a former partner at Ernst & Young LLP, tells of attending a high-level off-shore strategy meeting at which she was the sole woman among six men. Directing the meeting was a fifty-year-old man; of the other men, one-half were Janet's contemporaries, all forty-something. When Janet spoke, the meeting leader did not look at her. He did not acknowledge her comments. To him, she was both invisible and inaudible.

But her contemporaries did hear her. In fact, after a couple of them had noted aloud that "Janet's point is a good one," she "jumped up," as she herself put it, "took the magic marker, and said, 'May I suggest a framework within which to tackle this problem?' " Before the startled meeting leader could protest, Janet had moved quickly to the flip chart and was proceeding to lay out her ideas. It was those ideas that eventually carried the day—and drove the project to its eventual success and Janet to increased responsibility. But the lesson was not lost on her: Like the woman Bill coached, she was "blocked" in her attempt to

communicate simply because she is a woman. The lesson for successful women seeking the breakthrough to power? Grab the magic
marker, move right up to the flip chart, and say what you have to say.
Don't wait for acceptance—as Janet Green's international meeting
showed, you can't count on it off-shore any more than on-shore—and
don't wait, much less ask, for permission to speak. Just say it.

What's the reason women aren't communicating in the right way
in corporations? Why can't they get themselves heard? Certainly it's
not that women don't know what they're talking about. On the contrary: They sometimes tend to overwhelm the communication
process with the comprehensiveness of their knowledge. Take the case
of a financial services CFO who typically dragged a small army of files
and a mountain of slides to every meeting. But her CEO, a numbers
guy, just wanted a brief précis of the facts, a quick take on the core
issue, and a one-two-three set of recommendations. It wasn't until he
had noted her information overkill on her performance review that
she wised up. In fact, she still prepared enough back-up material to
crush Gibraltar, but the CEO didn't see it. For him, her presentations
were concise and to the point, no longer bogged down in the details
of her hard-won, very thorough knowledge—as displayed on numerous back-up slides.

Nor is the issue one of not knowing what the point is. Women are
as savvy as men about what's really at the heart of the matter. But they
have a tendency not to get to the point right away. Instead, they wan-
der toward it slowly and circuitously, explaining all the detours and
obstacles along the way, building a case. It's conversational foreplay—
but in the corporate environment, that isn't particularly sexy.

Partly, this tendency to delay getting to the point may just be conditioning. "Women have been trained since childhood to be less
direct," writes Judith Briles in *Gendertraps*[12]; young girls were traditionally taught to believe they would get more through coyness than
through directness. And partly, it may also be the point made at the
start of this chapter—that women simply gather and process infor-

mation differently from men. In fact, they approach the whole process of communicating in a different way.

One very senior and feisty investment banker recognizes that she constantly second-guesses herself—especially when she is the only woman in a room full of her male colleagues. As she tells it, "I tend to let the men speak first, so I'm sure I'll get it right. Even if the topic was breastfeeding, I would hold back to be sure I got it right. After all," she says, "it was more than fifteen years ago that I had my child."

Such second-guessing is a bad strategy from the start. If you question your own judgment—constantly and consistently—others will question it as well. You failed to learn self-confidence in school or at home? That was then; this is now. Speak for yourself.

MALE-FEMALE DIFFERENCES

Women tend to personalize communications. Put two women together, and in half an hour, they will know a lot about each other. Put two men together, and you may have half an hour of uncomfortable silence punctuated by a rundown of last night's sports scores. By the same token, women want to "nurture" the information they gather; they want to absorb it thoroughly and understand the rationale behind it before they commit to it and communicate it elsewhere. Men are more intuitive about communicating; they want to get the task done, and what passes through their minds as a way to get it done seems to them worth communicating.

Research shows that men are comfortable actually making things up. Asked for a particular financial figure, for example, a man will pluck a number from thin air and offer it in an authoritative and confident voice. A woman, by contrast, will confess that she does not know—and she'll probably go on to add that she hasn't triple-checked it, only gave it a last-minute review, only had time to be briefed by an assistant but has not herself seen every chart from which the figure comes, and so on,—giving the impression that she doesn't know what she's talking about, when in fact she more than likely knows it thoroughly, better than the men.

THREE STEPS

Communication is the fuel of power, and communicating well is at the heart of leadership. Think about it. Every great leader, whether of a nation or of a corporation, has had not only a great vision but an ability to communicate it. If, on your path to power, you are given a choice between a great vision and no ability to communicate it, and an ability to communicate with no vision to offer, take the latter—and hope that the vision will come to you.

To put yourself on the path to becoming a powerful leader, you need an approach to overcome the obstacles in the way of your communicating. The approach is threefold: (1) how to listen effectively, (2) how to be heard, and (3) how to be viewed as knowledgeable—as having the information that *is* power.

Step 1: The Art of Listening. Listening is key to every strategy in this book. You will adapt more easily, manage a line operation more astutely, bond with your boss more closely, and build a better power base if you learn how to listen. The same goes for the strategies still to come; whether the issue is marketing yourself, ratcheting up the content of your work, managing your career, multispecializing, capitalizing on your emotions, or acting like a leader, effective listening is an essential tool, one that senior-level people cannot afford to be without. It is critical to taking the power you deserve.

Yet study after study shows that people listen at about one-third of their ability. They lose a lot in that two-thirds they fail to use: accuracy of information, understanding, the ability to respond effectively and act purposefully. Effective listening—listening with all your capacity—ensures that you will receive fewer reporting errors, clarify attitudes, build rapport, hear the hidden messages, and improve your own credibility. All of these are important items on the power agenda.

In fact, listening well—and being perceived as a good listener—is one of the most powerful tools you can have in corporate life. The reason is simple: Corporations are filled with people. You get things done through people; equally, when you can't get things done, it's usually because people stand in the way. Listening well is an outstanding lubricant that can smooth your way through reluctant people. It is an almost magic elixir for spurring the energies of people to do something that might be good for you but is not necessarily advantageous for them. The old saying holds true: No one cares how much you know until they know how much you care. Nothing is more suited to showing you care than being able to listen.

One caveat: Listening well can take time. To a busy, impatient executive—someone like yourself, perhaps—the time can seem wasted. You're bright enough to catch on quickly to what the person is going to say; you're desperate to cut them off in mid-sentence and tell them to "get on with it." Don't. First, it's rude—and rudeness never won anyone's loyalty. Second, while your brain is thinking about how the meter is running, or preparing a reply to the person, or reliving the joke you heard last night, you just might be missing something important. Former Congresswoman Pat Schroeder of Colorado, now president and chief executive of the Association of American Publishers, brings to this issue a good politician's perspective. "So often I know where people are going, and I want to finish their sentences for them," Schroeder told the *Investor's Business Daily*.[13] "I've found it helps to say to myself, 'Slow down. *It's their turn.*' That way, I listen more patiently" [italics ours].

FIVE TIPS TO EFFECTIVE LISTENING

When we say *listen,* we're using the word as an action verb. There's nothing passive about this process. It's not a time to kick back; rather, it's a moment to zero in hard, as you put to work a string of mental skills. All those skills are aimed at a goal: to become the kind of listener people want to talk to, the kind of listener they naturally open up to. Remember Strategy 5 on politics? Information *is* power. You get information by listening. You listen well by practicing the following skills every time someone needs to talk to you.

1. Focus. Start by screening out all distractions. Even in the most hectic of settings, push into the background all the physical and psychological noise that has nothing to do with the person who's talking to you. The ringing phone, the ambient hum of business, the snatches of conversation of those two operations managers over near the copy machine are all barriers to the task at hand. Blank them out. Force yourself to attend to your interlocutor. Face him, look him in the eyes, put your mind right on him. Concentrate.

The words are foremost, of course, but that isn't all you should attend to. Pay attention to the whole package: the manner, the body language, whether the sound of the voice is casual or forced, committed or indifferent, posed or genuine. Go behind the speech to hear what's driving the speaker.

Then listen to every word he says.

2. Interpret. As you listen to the words, hear the meaning. What's *really* being said? Mentally define what you're listening to in your own terms; paraphrase it into your personal buzzwords. The nonverbal cues you pick up are as important as the words. What do they tell you? How do they add to or color or enrich the meaning? What emotional hot buttons can you sense in what you're hearing? In short, what is the message—and what is its significance to you?

3. Evaluate. Appraise what you hear. Calculate its worth. Is it true? likely? probable? interesting? something that should be acted upon or something to store away for potential use in the future? Evaluate the speaker as well: What are the strengths and weaknesses of his or her presentation—his or her ability as a communicator?

4. Validate. It's your turn to speak, but this is still the listening process. Your contribution to it here is to corroborate that you hear what's being said. In doing so, you're not approving your interlocutor's position or opinion or even the facts he or she has laid out. You are simply confirming to the person that they're getting through to you, that the message they mean to transmit is coming across.

Do it by simply giving back to the speaker his or her own words—without the evaluation that is quietly proceeding apace in your mind. "I hear your concern about rolling out the new product. I understand it may be difficult to meet the month-end target as a result." Period. You don't have to say more. If your speaker seems to want more, say the same thing over again in slightly different words. You're thus validating that you've heard the person. Let him keep going; spur him to elaborate further. The result just might be that he'll come up with a solution.

5. Respond with rapport. In fact, you can end your feedback right there—with a simple affirmation that you get the message. Or, you can respond—again by declaring your willingness to listen. Dig deeper, look for the common ground between your interlocutor and you. Coax the person to reveal more by showing that you're curious, that what they've said has struck you as interesting and important. Ask questions that help you understand more about the person, about his or her emotional needs, about the deeper implications of what was said. It's easy to decide that people who agree with us are brilliant; in the same way, it's easy to think that people who ask for more information on what we are thinking and feeling have the mark of a leader. So ask for more information; probe more deeply. It is leaders, after all, who help people solve problems by listening and asking questions.

Note that responding with rapport does not necessarily include agreeing with the person, making any kind of commitment, or saying anything substantive at all. Obviously, you may determine the situation calls for that. If it does, the strategy for making yourself heard should kick in.

Step 2: The Art of Presenting. The shelves of bookstores and libraries groan under the weight of works on business communications. Manuals and handbooks, quick how-to's and weighty scholarly tomes offer their varying perspectives, their expertise, their inside savvy. Almost all of them have something worthwhile to offer—whether it's advice on how to make a killer presentation or a set of rules on how to speak up at a meeting for the first time in your career or tips on how to talk your way to the top.

Our concern here, however, is much more basic. It's with the fundamentals of making yourself heard. Whatever the subject matter, whatever the circumstances, these fundamentals prevail. Whether you're making a presentation to the board of directors, chewing someone out, asking your boss for a raise, motivating your staff, having a one-on-one with a colleague who is also a rival, firing a subordinate, or taking a phone call from the chairman, following these ten basic steps will enable you to say what you need to say clearly and effectively enough that you can be confident you've been heard.

Of course, this assumes that you have something to say. Nothing is more quickly evident in the corridors of corporate power than what the *New Yorker* magazine used to call "The In-Love-With-The-Sound-of-Their-Own-Words Department." Participating in a conversation just to show that you have breath in your body when you actually have nothing to say may simply show that you're a fool—someone who talks in order to draw attention to herself. Do as your mother advised: If you have nothing to say, don't say anything.

TEN TIPS ON THE ART OF PRESENTING

Here are ten tips that will help you say what you need to say so that the person or people you're saying it to will hear it loud and clear. They include ten key questions to put to yourself and one simple formula for putting it all together. The questions first:

1. **Whom are you talking to?** The first step is to profile the person or people you're speaking to. We don't mean by this just an objec-

tive identification—an audience of 200, a conference of six managers superior to me, my chief of staff, my boss, twenty workers on the line. We mean: Who *are* they? What is their interest in whatever it is you will say to them? What will it do for them? In short, why should they listen to you?

Your audience—whether it contains one or one hundred—has hot buttons. If you're not sure what they are, find out. If your audience of one is the CEO, there will be lots of low-down about him that you can glean from conversations with others—if you listen well. If your audience of 100 is a group of conservative Muslim ayatollahs who believe women should be dressed in head-to-toe chadors, you'll both have to compromise a bit if you're going to be heard. It would be extremely important to know that ahead of time.

And that's the point. People often forget that a key word in the phrase "talking to someone" is the word *to*. You're not speaking in a vacuum. You're talking to living humans—many of whom may differ from you and may well disagree with you—and you have to talk to them in a way that will make them listen. For that to happen, you have to know who they are—not in minute detail, but with sufficient concreteness that you can connect with them.

What are their expectations? What's in it for them—that is, what will they take from your talk that will pique their interest or advance their interests?

2. What's the setting? Where will you be doing your communicating? Obviously, you'll speak differently among equals in a conference room from the way you would speak in giving a dinner speech at a professional conference. You would write differently in a quick email to your staff from the way you would compose a note to your boss or peer.

It isn't simply a matter of adjusting your tone, either. The total package must be appropriate to the setting. For the dinner speech to 300 people, you may need a polished script that you've rehearsed over and over on both hard copy and teleprompter, shoes that won't pinch your feet five minutes into your talk, and practice on timing if that opening joke is going to work. Remember an old technique: Take three breaths before you speak to steady your nerves.

For firing the subordinate, you want a private office, absolutely no interruptions, the performance review and complete documentation at hand, and a polished script of what to say that you've rehearsed over and over.

For a presentation to the board of directors or to a small senior-management group, be careful to rehearse ahead of time the Power-Point slides, overheads, or handouts you may be working from. Technology is a wonderful tool, but too much sizzle can fizzle. Remember that these things are "visual aids"; they're there to support and illustrate the points you're making. Don't rely on slides to carry your message for you.

Communicating is a stage performance writ small. Set the scene if you can; be aware of it if you can't.

3. What's your goal? What have you come here for? There's a reason. Perhaps you've come to inform. Or to instruct. Or to ask questions and learn. Or to gain approval and a green light on your project. Maybe your purpose is to persuade. Or to prove a point. Perhaps you're here to negotiate. Or just simply to win. Or all of the above. Whatever your purpose, articulate it to yourself so that it stays in the front of your mind once you begin talking or writing.

4. What do you want to say? Pause. Step back from the immediate situation. Now just think about what you're going to say. To fulfill your goal, what's the message that will work? What is the actual content of what you're communicating? What do you want your audience to know—what message do you want them to walk away with? Be focused—and refocus when you need to.

Before a meeting with her boss, Ann Reese, former CFO of ITT, would always ask herself this question: "If I were hit by a bus just after a meeting with my boss, what were the three things I had to make sure I told him?" She limited herself strictly to just three. You can, too.

Write them down—on the back of your hand, if you like, to re-create the classic cheat sheet. Carry it into the meeting with you. Refer to it as needed.

Don't burden the audience with too many details. Business communicators—regardless of gender—far too often miss the mark because they are talking from an altitude of 80,000 feet or because they drill too deep into technical issues. Put yourself in your audience's shoes and talk directly to the points that make sense to them.

Remember, of course, that what counts is not what your message does to the listener but what the listener does with your message. Perhaps your listener is the decision-maker who can kill your project. The last thing you want to do is befuddle him with a mass of unnecessary detail or extraneous anecdote. What, precisely, must he take from this presentation? Whatever it is, make sure you deliver it—and hold the details and anecdotes in reserve.

Remember too that you are part of the message. Your manner, your personality, your confidence will all be communicated along with what you say. Plan and rehearse that part of the message ahead of time as well.

5. What are the facts that support what you want to say? How well you know your subject matter really comes through in presentations. This is not the time or place to wing it—or to give superficial answers during the Q&A. So anticipate questions, know what you need to know, and bring it with you in your brain. But bring supporting evidence as well. You won't need stacks of material—quantity isn't what will wow them—just the facts that back up what you've come to say or that form the basis for the question you're asking. The point is to have the supporting evidence with you, at the ready—facts appropriate to your message, facts that will highlight the message and make it more credible or interesting.

6. Tell them what you're going to tell them, tell them, then tell them what you've told them. This fundamental formula of speechmaking makes a good working paradigm for any form of communication. Tell your audience why you're communicating to them, artic-ulate your message, support what you're saying with facts as needed, then summarize what you've just said.

There is almost never any need for a speech or presentation to take longer than ten minutes. For one thing, it's hard for most audi-ences to sit still for any longer than that, much less absorb anything important—one of the downsides of the time we spend watching commercial television. Ten minutes is also all that most corporate executives have time for in a one-on-one. Jewelle Bickford, Senior Managing Director at Rothschild, Inc., says she was lucky to be the only girl among three children. With two brothers, she learned quickly that if she wanted air time, she had better speak up and get her point across fast.

The best way to avoid the kind of speech that makes the audience repeatedly check its watch is to steer clear of complexity. Spoken detail is the enemy of retention. The deeper you go, the less people will remember. Try to make three words do the work of seven. It isn't easy— "I would have written a short letter," wrote the famed eighteenth-century lexicographer Samuel Johnson, "but I didn't have time"—but if the three words are well-chosen, it's far more effective.

When you've finished saying what you have to say, stop talking. Chances are you've been heard. But if for some reason you haven't gotten your message across by now, no amount of rehash, static, or empty words is going to do it.

7. **Engage your audience.** You just *think* there are 500 people in the audience, all staring at you, waiting to hear what you have to say, challenging you not to bore them. In fact, the whole trick in making a speech is to have a conversation with one person . . . at a time. A good speaker engages the audience by "spotting" first that person there, then that one over there, then the one up in the balcony over there, and now the woman right down front here on the right . . . and so on.

Now have the conversation. Ask a question, tell a story, poke fun at yourself, ask for a show of hands, acknowledge the response. Let the audience know you know they're there; let them know you are listening to them. Break down the wall between you and your audience.

The same thing goes when you are making a presentation to the chairman, CFO, and COO. Look each of them in the eye, make your case: It's a conversation, and it's your turn to speak.

Dorothy Sarnoff, a veteran communications coach who trained many politicians, world leaders, CEOs, and celebrities—and who also starred in the original Broadway production of *The King and I*—has a wonderful formula for gearing up for a speech or presentation. Her advice is to say the following to yourself before "going onstage:" *I am happy to be here . . . I am happy you, the audience, are here . . . I have something to say . . . and I know what I'm talking about.*

8. No excuses, no apologies, no equivocation. Corporate lingo is rife with circumlocution, shuffling, fencing, and downright doublespeak. For that very reason, boldness makes people sit up and take notice. Speak with directness and authority, and people believe you're in command of the facts and should be listened to. The worst thing in the world is to hear somebody weasel into a point, or "suggest" a solution, or apologize for not having dotted every 'i' and crossed every 't' in the research. "Although we weren't able to check all the studies, based on the bulk of the reports received to date, we think there are several courses of action that might be useful"—the implication is that the speaker is already looking for cover on every possible score. The result? The audience is instantly dubious.

Women do this more than men—and not only in corporate life. A great study by the husband-and-wife team of David and Myra Sadker at the American University of Education shows that boys call out answers to teachers' questions eight times more often than girls do. And guess what: Boys receive more teacher attention than girls do. The implication is clear: A bold bid for attention gets you attention. The Sadkers also studied the grown-up versions of these test subjects, asking professional men and women about mistakes they had made in their professional lives and what they had done about them. The women in the study remembered their bloopers with angst and self-recrimination. The men could barely remember any mistakes—except maybe one or two that were someone else's fault.

"I am in earnest," wrote William Lloyd Garrison in 1831, "I will not equivocate—I will not excuse—I will not retreat a single inch—and I will be heard!" Follow that lead.

9. Pay attention to packaging. Presentation matters. How you dress, how you walk, how you present yourself to those around you speak as loud and clear as your words and thus affect how your message is perceived. When former Texas Governor Ann Richards addressed the 1997 Women's Summit in San Francisco, she began by asserting that "if you want to be treated like a professional, then you should stop wearing those stupid ponytails to work." Take it a step further: If you're making a speech to a bunch of hard-nosed businessmen, show them a hard-nosed businesswoman who knows what she is saying and how to say it.

How should you dress? Appropriately—for your industry and for the situation. When Avon Products' President Andrea Jung dresses for the podium, she looks stylish, glamorous, and utterly businesslike—and it all enhances her company's message and products.

Some things are clearly inappropriate: Noisy bracelets and flashy clothes will drown out what you have to say whatever the situation. If you're in doubt about your own sense of dress, hire an image consultant to help you select the right style and colors for your body type. Don't let your clothes or your jewelry distract your audience from the real message—you and what you're saying.

10. Think on your feet—calmly. You've just delivered a presentation to senior management, and the CFO asks a question you cannot answer. What do you do? To collect your thoughts, press for clarification—"What aspect of the issue did you want me to address?" or "Are you referring to the market segmentation plan?" or something that touches on what's on his mind. Give some answer if you can; if you cannot, you can always say that the issue the CFO has raised is a great point and one worth looking into further and you'll get back to him on it.

Or, the COO wants to know if you've "gotten any input from JFI." JFI? What, you are thinking as your mind races through the possibilities, is a JFI? Joint Force on Integration? Job Forms Inventory? Just Fake It? No. Ask the COO to "remind me again what JFI stands for." It may even make the COO feel good that he has used jargon not everyone is familiar with. It confirms his singularity.

The point is to not personalize your lack of an instant comeback. It's one of those situations in which women really do need to be more like men. Men roll with the punches. Women take the punches. Men are perfectly happy speaking on topics about which they may know nothing. Women tend to become defensive when they don't know something.

When she was First Lady, Hillary Rodham Clinton made a major faux pas at a press conference—and followed it with a major recovery. She was talking about a woman whose son had died from lead poisoning, or so Mrs. Clinton had been told. In fact, as someone in the audience pointed out, the boy had not died at all. Without skipping a beat, Hillary simply said: "Thank God he's okay. Praise the Lord for that." She didn't become flustered, didn't stumble, was not paralyzed by embarrassment, did not internalize the mistake. She put it behind her and went forward. The lesson? When you're on the spot unexpectedly, deal with it quickly and move on.

Sometimes, however, a question or comment on your presentation is actually a way of trying to shoot you down. When that happens, turn it back to the person making the comment and ask for specifics. "What precisely do you object to?" you might ask, or "Why, specifically, do you object? Has this issue been a problem before? How?" Put the monkey on the other guy's back—and don't back away. Hold his feet to the fire.

Here are a couple of worksheets to help you prepare for your next presentation, whether it's a meeting with your direct reports, a slide show for the CEO, or a keynote speech at an industry conference. First, map out the purpose and content of your communication; then, make sure you've covered all the preparation bases—before you say a word. Use a chart like the one shown in Figure 6.1 to make sure you have a focused and concise presentation which will get you the result you want.

The next step involves practice, practice, and more practice. Use a checklist like the one in Figure 6.2 to ensure you are prepared and have internalized your presentation.

Step 3: How to Be Viewed as Knowledgeable. It's a truism that knowledge is power. Communicating the sense that you possess knowledge is thus a key step on the path to power. The bottom line on this is simple: You've got to know your stuff. By that we mean you've got to know your business and the dynamics that drive it both internally and externally, what it takes to grow both the top and the bottom lines, the organization's products and services, how the firm stacks up against its competition, how decisions are made, and what's important to managers. Come to the table with less than that, and it's only a matter of time before you're cast in a superficial light.

Figure 6.1 Communications Map.

Who is the audience?	
What is my goal?	
What are my three key points?	
What key facts support these points?	
What message do I want to leave with the audience?	
What action or result do I want from the audience?	
How do I feel about my presentation?	
After much more practice, how do I feel about my presentation?	

Figure 6.2 The Prepresentation/Prespeech Checklist.

Key Presentation Points	Action Item
I've done my homework on the audience	
I've checked to see if the occasion or protocol requires prepared remarks, notes, or visuals	
I've focused on getting to my message quickly	
I have learned how to breathe and how to project my voice	
I use humor to make my points	
I have rehearsed and timed the presentation/speech	
I have allowed time for Q&A	
I have planned appropriate clothing, accessories, jewelry—the right "packaging"	
I have prepared the visuals and cued them to the script	
I have anticipated likely questions and know how I will handle them	
I can boil down the gist of my presentation/speech to three key points	
I know how and when I will engage the audience	

Why? Because as a woman seeking power, you're still swimming against the tide, still fighting a historical perception that women get to the top for reasons *other* than what they know—for tokenism perhaps, or legalism, politics, goods looks and/or sex, to name a few.

So what exactly should you know? The short answer is enough to be recognized as business-wise. You need to be fluent in the language of your company and your business as well as your competition and the world at large. Corporations operate globally and you must too. The following is a basic eight-point checklist.

EIGHT TIPS ON BEING KNOWLEDGEABLE

1. **Know how you and your department impact the bottom line.** Know your numbers—what you contribute to the business and what you cost the business. Know how you interrelate with other areas in terms of revenue generation and expenses.

2. **Know your organization's balance sheet.** If you work for a publicly held company you should know its vital statistics—income, sales, cash flow, earnings per share, number of employees—whatever the key performance barometers are that measure the financial fitness of your firm. Know how market analysts value your company and the market's perceptions of your industry. If you don't know these numbers, consult your annual report. It's all there in the back of the book, on the company website, or available through EDGAR, the federal government's file on all public companies. If you don't under-stand the numbers or the terms, don't be embarrassed to admit it—you're not alone. Take a financial course for nonfinancial professionals. Or talk to the finance people below the CFO, controller, and treasurer—the people who actually crunch the numbers. You would be surprised how flattered they would be to offer their advice; they are an untapped resource loaded with valuable information. Professional organizations like the American Management Association offer excellent classes that will get you up to speed on the basic measurement tools in short order.

3. **Know how your company stacks up against competitors.** If you're the Pfizer of your industry, how do you compare to your industry's equivalent of Merck or Johnson & Johnson? Where does the company stand in its market category? If you're work-ing for a large-cap company, where does it fit in the Fortune 500? If your company is privately held, how does it size up in your field or industry?

4. **Know the operations.** That is, know how work flows through your organization and how one department impacts another. This is critical because it is a road map for getting things done, and it's essential to be seen as someone who knows how to get things done. It also shows how information flows through your company, and you want to be seen as someone who knows how to get a message across.

5. **Know your company's products and/or services.** You'd be surprised at how many people at senior levels—particularly those in wide-ranging multinationals with broad product portfolios—don't know what their firms do companywide. This doesn't mean you have to know every single product in every single country. But you should know the market segments in which your firm competes and the clients your organization serves. Ask the marketing department for a market segmentation analysis showing your company's target client base by product lines.

6. **Know the trends that affect your business.** No organization exists in a vacuum. And neither can you. In a global economy, worldwide business trends and dynamics are more important than ever. Your organization can be impacted by interest rates set in Washington, exchange rates that float, the health of regional economies, producer prices, wholesale prices, retailer activities. It could be affected by fashion trends, demographic or lifestyle trends, seasonal holidays, demand for commodity products, political factors, even the weather. You need to be aware of just about all of it. Read at least a few of the major business publications—*Wall Street Journal, Fortune, Business Week, Forbes, Barrons, Investors Business Daily*—and whatever particular trade publication covers your industry. Most have websites, making it easier than ever to access these resources.

7. **Know the corporate vision, mission, values, and longer-term objectives.** What drives the organization? What operational issues are important to the management team? Every company has a focal point, often centered on a specific theme, that sum-

marizes the firm's direction or goals. Know what the corporation has published; even more to the point, figure out how your business fits into the overall corporate scheme and how it thus relates with other areas. Is the cross-sell of products recognized and rewarded in the company?

8. **Know how decisions are made.** What is the process by which decisions are arrived at? Where do you go to get things done? Which buttons do you push when you get there?

If and when you know all this, you won't have to show it. It will show itself as you communicate—and you'll be viewed as a person who has the kind of knowledge that really is power.

STRATEGY 7

Marketing: Brand You!

Bill: As a man, I can say that I do think men probably are overvalued in corporations, women inherently undervalued. Do you agree?

Janice: Yes, and I think it's because men have an easier time demonstrating confidence in their own distinctive abilities. It started with our socialization differences when we were children.

Bill: Confidence and a willingness to promote those abilities through sports and such.

Janice: Exactly. Women tend to think people can mind-read their accomplishments, or that others will guess instinctively how great the woman's accomplishments have been.

Bill: It doesn't happen that way, however. Women have to learn to create a signature style and market it. Aggressively.

Janice: Absolutely. After all, if you don't market yourself, others won't either.

Contemporary jargon calls it "branding," and the jargon is right-on: Brand You! It means you must create a brand for yourself, then sell it. It's marketing, it's public relations, it's about personality as well as accomplishment, and it is absolutely essential in today's business environment.

Why? Because it's a knowledge-based world; it's a performance-driven arena; process counts more than function. You can do your job well . . . and do it well . . . and continue to do it well. And as New Yorkers say, "that and a buck-fifty will get you on the subway." Doing one job well is not nearly enough in today's world. If you're going to move on, move out, and move up to power, you must not only create value, you must *demonstrate* that you create value.

Men seem instinctively to have a sense of their own distinctive worth. More to the point, their willingness to speak up—even, as we saw in Strategy 6, when they may not fully know what they're talking about—is one aspect of their confidence when it comes to self-marketing. If you're comfortable contriving a fact out of thin air, then chances are you won't have any qualms about tooting your own horn.

Women, on the other hand, are still proving themselves, still stepping gingerly into the higher reaches of corporate power, still not quite sure what the next step should be. With the men around them continuing to question what all these women are doing in what was once their exclusive clubhouse, it's no wonder women question it, too. If you're dubious about your very legitimacy, it's hard to promote your distinctive value.

Yet promoting your distinctive value is a key item on the power agenda. When you're out to get the power, if you don't leave your mark, you can lose the trail altogether—and end up lost in the corporation. The lesson? Be visible—and be bold.

SCENARIO:

Martha T. had been interviewed by the president of the company. She believed she had made it clear during the interview that she wanted the job; she believed she was qualified. Two days later, screwing her courage to the sticking point, she phoned the president, reminded him of their interview, of her qualifications, and of her eagerness for the job, then said: "You'll be making a big mistake if you don't hire me."

He hired her.

FOUR STEPS

Here's a simple, four-step approach for identifying and planning a Brand You marketing campaign—and for executing the campaign with high visibility.

Step 1: Do Market Research. Before you can market the product—you—you have to know the perceptions there are of you both within and outside the organization.

One way to find out is to ask. Take a tip from former New York Mayor Ed Koch, who used to walk around the city, buttonholing its citizens and demanding: "How'm I doing?" But be careful. In the corporate world, you put people in a powerful position when you ask how you're perceived. They may then talk to each other and start supporting each other's views; pretty soon, you may find yourself saddled with labels you never deserved. Look for well-balanced individuals who are secure with who they are and where they are in life—maybe your boss, some peers. Check out who is trusted to maintain a confidence. There are probably only a few. Seek out these individuals and get their feedback.

And if you're not clear about what they're telling you, ask for clarification.

Don't show offense at what you hear and, most of all, don't become defensive. Take the feedback, sort through it, and test it on family and close friends to see what's accurate, what's not, and what perceptions need to be changed.

Another way to find out how you're perceived is through your own intuition. Women are supposed to have particularly acute intuitive capabilities. Now's the time to use them. Trust those instincts. Does it seem to you you're being invited to fewer meetings? Are the assignments entrusted to you less and less important? Was your bonus less than you expected? Greater? How do your subordinates react to you? Are you liked? Listened to? Sought out? What about departmental meetings—are you recognized, listened to, paid attention to? Put together the clues to get an idea of how you're perceived.

In addition, of course, pay attention to the formal evaluations of your performance—your annual review, 360 evaluations, or whatever else your organization relies on to get information on you. The 360 feedback is becoming an increasingly common mechanism for evaluating performance and weeding out executives with people problems. It's extremely helpful to corporate management to find—and derail—those executives who simply cannot lead people or build relationships with their colleagues. If the department resembles a revolving door or if the executive goes through secretaries like Sherman through Georgia, the 360 feedback finds it. But beware! Here again the double standard raises its ugly head. A man can chew up people and be seen as a hard-driving go-getter. A woman will be viewed as a poor manager.

Once you've gotten your feedback and done your market research, map it the way consumer products companies map their products—as a set of features and benefits. What features distinguish you from others, and what product benefits do you provide that others want? Maybe a distinguishing feature is that you are laserlike in your problem-solving skills. The benefit to those you work with is that it gives you a particular ability to handle multiple issues and make quick decisions on problems that others need solved. Create your own features and benefits model using the worksheet in Figure 7.1.

Step 2: Create Your Tagline.   You know all those stories about making pitches to Hollywood producers? Pretend they're true. Now pretend that a blank piece of paper is a Hollywood producer. Pitch yourself to him. What's the three-sentence essence of you that he can take to the bank? In twenty-five words or less, what value can you create for him that he can't find anywhere else for the price? Give him the tagline. Show him your trademark.

What's a pitch? A tagline? A trademark? You know them when

Figure 7.1 My Features/Benefits Model
Product = You!

	My Product Features (What distinguishes me from others?)	My Product Benefits (How do I make an impact?)	Possible Tagline (for me based on this information)
What people in the organization say about me			
What people outside the organization say about me			
What my last performance review highlighted			
What I see in myself			
My three value-added bottom-line accomplishments			
What I did politically or for an outside charitable/civic organization			

you see them. They're everywhere. "The Document Company." Golden arches. The swoosh on a pair of sneakers. All of these speak to you. And they don't just tell you names—Xerox, McDonald's, Nike. They push a button inside you, and a whole tape begins playing—of feelings, experiences, appetites.

The pitch, tagline, and trademark are the outward expressions of a brand. And brand is the thing that sets you apart. It's the distinctively different value you bring to the corporation. Step 2 is to find it.

Start with your features/benefits model and take it a step further to come up with a bragging-rights model: the accomplishments, innovations, projects, ideas, achievements that you know contributed distinctive value. These are the things you're most proud of—unabashedly so, rightly, deservedly, justifiably so. Put them on paper using the worksheet in Figure 7.2 as an example.

The features/benefits model tells you what's salable about you; the bragging-rights model tells your key accomplishments; now it's time to show how good you are at overcoming challenges. Fill in a CAR worksheet like the one in Figure 7.3—challenges, actions, results. What were the challenges you faced, actions you took, and the direct results that really distinguish you from the crowd?

Take a look at all three worksheets. Read them over a few times. Distill the core message of each into a single sentence. Put them together. You've got your three-sentence tagline pitch. Write it down on a sheet of paper.

How does it sound? Work on it till it says what you believe it ought to convey: the special value that is you.

Figure 7.2   Bragging-Rights Model.

My Accomplishments: What I am most proud of:
Inside the organization
Outside the organization
Bottom-line tagline: "I am someone who. . . ."

Figure 7.3 Challenges, Actions, Results.

Key Challenges I Have Handled	Actions I Took	Direct Results of My Efforts

Step 3: Create a Brochure.　We mean this literally. Most word processing programs today—including Microsoft Word—offer brochure "wizards" that will lead you step-by-step through the creation of your own brochure, including clip art and graphics. Use anything and everything that can flesh out and enrich your image as someone valuable to the organization.

Its aim is to convince the reader of the substantial and distinctive benefits you can bring to him and his organization. To do that, your brochure should set out your own personal unique selling proposition. It is your showcase of past accomplishments—not just any past accomplishments randomly thrown onto paper, but those past accomplishments that evidence the future-forward value you will bring to the reader. In short, you've handled distinctive challenges in the past; you can do so for the reader in the future. Your brochure convinces the reader of that.

. . . except that your Brand You brochure is a working document that no one but you need ever see. It will, of course, be the basis of the Brand You resume you may wish to write, but its primary usefulness is as a strategic step in the campaign to market yourself. Use it as a reference work. Keep it up to date; adapt it to the changing needs of your changing organization.

Here's a suggested outline for the contents of the Brand You brochure, but the best bet is to craft your own:

TITLE—THE TAGLINE FOR BRAND YOU

 I. *What the organization needs now*
 II. *The Brand You unique selling proposition—the distinctive value you can add, expressed in CAR format*
 III. *The Brand You features/benefits model—attributes of your excellence*
 IV. *The Brand You bragging-rights model—what you've done that made a difference, how it shows you will make a difference in the future*
 V. *Re-cap—the Brand You pitch to the Hollywood producer*

Step 4: The Campaign.   You've identified your brand. You've translated your unique selling proposition into a lively sales-oriented document, a real brochure. In short, you have the tools you need. Now you have to go out there and market the product.

That's what this is—a marketing campaign. If the project were a widget, you would know precisely what is at stake: Increase the widget's market share, revenues, and profitability, and you can look forward to a promotion. You would also know precisely how to go about marketing the widget. The basic how-to doesn't change simply because the product is you.

SCENARIO:

Maria V. was not particularly restless in her job, but when she heard of an opening in Global Client Sales (GCS), she was interested. It would be a lateral move, with no particular advancement or promotion; in fact, it would require Maria to learn a new area, and it would likely take her time to come up to speed on the learning curve. Nevertheless, she sensed that it would make strategic sense to get GCS experience—if she could sell herself. The question was how to go after the job, since she would never be an obvious choice for it, was doing well in her current position, and was presumed to be content where she was.

Maria researched the open position, then prepared a brochure that matched Brand Maria not to the job but to the organization's management needs as she saw them. She asked for a meeting with the head of HR and the senior manager to whom the head of GCS would report and gave them a detailed, determined, lively presentation based on her brochure. The challenges, actions, and results she described had little to do with globality, clients, or sales, but the accomplishments she chose to address showed that she was a woman who could motivate sluggish troops, restore flagging organizations to new life, and ratchet overall performance to a new level—her very own brand identity. As she pointed out—first to herself in her brochure, then to the meeting participants in her presentation—that was precisely what GCS needed. Maria's marketing campaign worked. She sold both managers on herself—and got the job.

What distinguishes the marketing campaign for Brand You from a marketing campaign for a widget or any other product is that everything you do is a marketing opportunity. Every meeting, every memo, every assignment you've either asked for or had handed to you is a potential point of sale, POS. And you can and should promote yourself at every POS.

You've got a one-on-one with the CFO? Don't just wow him with the work you've done in preparation; make sure he knows about the distinctive value you brought to the work. And listen to his comments, get his input, make him feel important.

You've been asked to speak at a conference? Don't just take pains to ensure that your boss and the legal department vet your speech ahead of time; take time afterwards to send a summary of the speech, along with the nice press coverage you received, to key opinion-makers in every important constituency in the organization.

It's important to remember, however, that the Brand You marketing campaign is not aimed solely at the movers and shakers. You're not only after the next job or the next leap up the power ladder, you're also—always—in search of raving fans from any and every corner of the corporation. Why? Because a cadre of people who think you're terrific establishes a tone, an aura that follows you wherever you go. Marketing Brand You gives people a sense that you have a signature style they like to be around. They may not even know what job you hold or what function you fulfill in the organization, but they know you have a distinctive personality that makes them feel good. And making people feel good at every level of the organization is one of those resources you'll need to draw on one of these days, for some purpose or other. People may soon forget what you did and what you said, but they will long remember how you made them feel.

The bottom-line on marketing Brand You? Nobody else can do it nearly as well as you can.

ELEVEN TIPS ON HOW TO LEAVE YOUR MARK

1. If your internal activities are not helping you achieve visibility within the organization, try going outside. Write an op-ed piece, join the chorus, get on the board of an organization or charity where people will help spread the word back to your company. In today's world, we are all connected by those famous six degrees of separation. With enough overlaps, your reputation will be reinforced by many influential people inside and outside the company.

2. Making speeches or teaching a course is a great way to get credit for expertise, add luster to your professional resume, and set yourself up for additional requests to address other groups. It's also a way of standing out from the crowd—and it's a super credit on your Brand You brochure!

3. Remember that word of mouth is one of the most powerful forces around. That's why you want raving fans everywhere in the corporation—among subordinates, superiors, and colleagues—not to mention among customers.

4. When you volunteer for an assignment in the corporation, do it *strategically.* Raise your hand for every project on the calendar and you will soon get a reputation as a busybody or, worse, as

the klutz who'll do everybody's grunt work. Choose projects, task forces, committees, chores that will get you noticed where it can do you some good. Remember: Visibility is the aim, not just more work.

5. Your reputation is sacrosanct and key to your brand. Do nothing to impair your reputation because to repair it may be near to impossible.

6. Take credit and give credit. Share magnanimously with others in celebrating their accomplishments. It enhances your brand identity.

7. Be consistent and predictable. People want to be able to rely on your features and benefits for the long-term.

8. Share your expertise and help others to be the best that they can be. Teaching is the role of every great leader.

9. Laugh at yourself and others will recognize you are human, approachable, and likeable.

10. Seek advice from others. Everyone likes to be acknowledged for what they know, and you will get a lot of great information as well as a new fan.

11. If you get "bad press" for something, take a tip from Johnson & Johnson facing the Tylenol disaster: React positively to negative news by facing and correcting the problem.

Responsibility: Be Significant, Dump the Insignificant

Janice*: Absolutely. I took my turn doing the more menial tasks. And I did it thinking it would get me more responsibility.

Bill*: We all do menial tasks now and again to show we're team players. That's part of the game, and it's a part everyone has to play from time to time.

Janice*: Yes, but the problem for women is that they raise their hands too often. They're looking for approval, recognition, to feel needed, or maybe just to demonstrate yet again that they can be team players. But the bottom line is that they end up doing things that don't matter.

Bill*: The consequence of volunteering for or accepting small-bore tasks is that you get a reputation for doing so—and then you end up doing the small stuff that doesn't count.

Janice*: But there isn't enough time as it is. Women need to focus on the stuff that will get them to the seat of power.

Most people will agree that it's women who get assigned the insignificant tasks in the corporation: a seat on the just-for-show task force that's "studying" how best to communicate strategy, authorship of a report on "changing demographics in the clerical population," and of course that perennial classic—taking notes at the senior officers' meeting. Research confirms that when it comes to all those extra assignments corporate executives are typically required to undertake, it's men who get the juicy prime cut and women who get the leftovers. As one of the women interviewed for this book wryly and eloquently put it: "As men keep score, stuff that doesn't get noticed is not a man's job."

SCENARIO:

The head of corporate marketing for a well-known consumer products firm was concerned that the in-house employee newsletter, the responsibility of the HR department, was published only sporadically and with meager content—as if it were an unimportant afterthought. He met with the HR director, who confirmed that he had more important things to do; so he approached Elizabeth G., who ran marketing communications, a typical "female ghetto" slot but one that she hoped to use for its high-profile visibility. Elizabeth was interested; done right, she thought, the newsletter could "cover" all the firm's businesses and extend her own exposure. She also believed passionately that positive employee communications could contribute to corporate branding, and that the newsletter could be part of that effort. She decided to talk it over with her division head. He asked her a single question: "Does the chairman read the newsletter?" The answer was no. Now Elizabeth saw her choice as either turning down the newsletter assignment or devoting the requisite time and resources to making it a publication the chairman *would* read. At that particular point in her career, Elizabeth determined there were better ways to establish her own significance. She declined the responsibility. There's still no in-house employee newsletter at the firm, and Elizabeth is finding other ways to make waves in marketing communications.

THE NURTURE TRAP

Why do the insignificant assignments "naturally" fall into women's laps? One reason is that those laps are accustomed to receiving the stubbed toe, the failing grade, the disappointment. Yes, most women have an innate ability to nurture—psychologically and physiologically—and one way they do that is to accept what others will not.

Then, of course, the others resent them for it.

In addition, women pay attention to certain things to which men are generally indifferent, and these things tend to involve environment, setting, the features of the nest. Women not only focus on the agenda for the upcoming client event. But they also are concerned about the decor for the cocktail reception and dinner, the mementos the customers will take away with them, the design of the certificate that will be ceremonially presented to the customer board member who's retiring this year. Women are used to thinking creatively about these sorts of things. It's what they've been doing in the family environment for thousands of years. In the corporate environment, however, the image has a negative impact: The women come off as big sister or as Mom—the last thing men want to see in their colleagues and rivals. At the same time, the men who run today's corporations want what the creative thinking women can give and are perfectly content to leave such things to women; in fact, they rely on women to handle these kinds of details.

Davia Temin, president of Temin and Company, a marketing and communications firm, puts it well: "Men's views of women are that the women are there to help them succeed," she told us in an interview. "Most of the men I've worked with and for had wives at home taking care of all the housekeeping items for them. Then they see women in business, and they just think that while women may have responsible jobs, they will also handle some of the less important stuff."

SPEND TIME GETTING THE CREDIT, NOT GETTING IT PERFECT

Perhaps as an offshoot of the nurturing instinct, women tend to work very hard at dotting every "i" and crossing every "t." In so many aspects of their lives and their working lives, as we've pointed out so many times in this book, women concentrate on all the details, and they insist on getting every single one of them just right before they'll consider a job finished. In corporate life, however, that's not necessarily what gets you noticed; it's not necessarily what's considered valuable. Work on what is important and getting that perfect. Delegate the rest with the necessary follow-up to ensure your team gets it perfect.

SCENARIO:

It was a four-day conference for customers from all over the world, a once-a-year extravaganza under the direct management of the CIO, who named Melanie D., an IT project manager, as his "detail person" on the task. The task was all details, and Melanie handled every one of them: concept, planning, the agenda, the key speakers, presenters, hosts, staging, production, securing the site, arranging all transportation, lodging, meals, entertainment, recreation, spa activities, breaks, snacks, downtime. It was a massive job, requiring months of time, on-your-feet decision-making, direct weekly reports to the CIO, regular memos to the CEO, press relations, customer contact, meeting and greeting the politicians, bankers, businesspeople, and VIPs who were speakers or guests.

The conference was a phenomenal success. In the conference program, which she had also produced, edited, and for the most part written, Melanie had been listed as "coordinator." At the last session on the last day, however, when the company CEO was delivering his wrap-up speech, he asked for "a special round of applause for the individual who made this conference possible." To wild cheering, he named his male CIO.

Davia Temin has conceived and directed many such conferences and agrees that women need to be sure they are listed on the program; the pat on the back with no recognition is unacceptable. "I've powdered more bald heads for guys that were going to be on camera," says Temin, "and I don't mind doing that—but I like my due too."

"Don't mind doing it. . . ." Far too many women don't mind doing it, but far too many forget to get their due.

Women can't and shouldn't "de-nature" themselves. They can't and shouldn't stifle their nurturing instincts. Both corporate America and the world at large will be the worse for it if they do. They shouldn't stifle the impulse to be team players, either, or to show eagerness for the work.

What they should do is show judgment. Discrimination. Selectivity. Strategic thinking. Of course you will continue to take on delegated assignments. You will even volunteer for some. But they will be assignments that will gain you a payoff. Maybe it's a step upward. Or visibility. Or the chance to learn an area with which you're unfamiliar—or a skill you really ought to have. No matter how small it is, a task that gains you a personal career advantage is not insignificant. It is not menial. Where such tasks are concerned, your response should be: Bring it on! For all other extra assignments, the answer should be a strategic no.

Here's a three-step approach for getting the former and putting the kibosh on the latter.

THREE STEPS

Step 1: Draw the Line. There are significant tasks, assignments, jobs, and commissions—and there are insignificant tasks, assignments, jobs, and commissions. Starting now, you no longer do what's insignificant or unimportant in the scheme of corporate goals. Instead, you work on what is important and get that perfect. Then you delegate the rest with the necessary follow-up to ensure your team gets it right.

How do you tell the difference between the significant and the insignificant? Here's a ten-point checklist that lets you draw the line between the menial and the major, between what's beneficial and what's banal. Remember: You're looking for career advantage; every decision must be a strategic one. Therefore, every time you're confronted by an assignment, or by the possibility of volunteering for a task, ask yourself these questions:

1. **Am I new to this job, company, department, area?** If so, perhaps taking on the assignment can be an opportunity to meet people, learn the landscape, establish your own identity. If you have been with the company, is this a new learning opportunity for you to take advantage of?

2. **Do I have the skill, knowledge, resources that are critical to successfully doing this task?** If not, can you get them? Are you being treated the same as others at your level?

3. **Will this assignment build respect for me?** It's a dull, boring, but necessary task. It will be tedious, even difficult to do. It will take time and patience and won't add anything to your resume. But it just might gain you respect. And the respect you gain might just be worth having.

4. **Is the task worth the time?** How long will the job last? If it will take longer than six months, you don't have time for it. Ancillary tasks need to have a faster turnaround—and a quicker payback. Unless this is a major project that supports a significant corporate objective, it may be more about research than results.

5. **Does it give me exposure?** Figure out who will see this task— not just its results but the process as well. Measure the assignment's potential impact on the organization. To whom will you be reporting? With whom will you work? What can those people do for you over the course of time? The assignment may be light as air, but the contacts you make and the visibility you achieve could make it all worth it. On the other hand, as one senior-level woman told us, "being a bulldozer for stuff that is not getting the chairman's attention has no payback. In fact, it has a silent boomerang effect. You don't even know what hit you, but all of a sudden, you're not in the loop, people don't think of you as a strategic thinker, you're labeled as someone

who focuses on details that have little significance and should have been handled by someone at a much lower level. All this—and you don't know what hit you."

6. **Is the assignment linked to the business?** So many of the task forces, studies, committees, and working groups formed in corporate life are just so much applesauce. If you're going to spend time in superficial tongue-wagging, make sure the end product is linked to the business.

7. **How will I be rewarded?** Simple enough: What do you get as a result of doing this job, being on this task force, and so on? What's the payoff? Is it going to be worth your time, effort, energy, involvement? Will it get you to the next level, give you visibility, count at bonus time?

8. **Can the assignment *become* significant?** Sure, this looks like just another specious bit of insubstantial make-work. But maybe, just maybe, it might turn into something of real substance—something that others may notice and find useful, or something that you yourself can learn from and profit by.

9. **Can I *make it* significant?** Maybe the task really *is* insubstantial make-work. Can you get kudos for making it a significant solution to a long-standing problem? Is there a by-product that will cure another ailment? That makes it all the more susceptible to being turned into a vehicle for some other purpose: Yours—if you take it over and manage it right.

10. **What are the politics?** Figure out who needs to have this job done—insignificant though its content may be. Or, figure out who's going to be relieved that someone else is doing it. What power base do you enter by doing it? Can you build your own power base by doing it? Politics alone might draw an insignificant task over the line, making it highly significant indeed.

If there are more minuses than pluses on your checklist, or if the minuses seem to outweigh the pluses even if they don't outnumber them, think hard about taking on the assignment. Only a responsibility that will get you where you want to go is a responsibility worth undertaking. Be strategically selective.

Step 2: To Say No, Don't Say No. How do you say no once your ten-point checklist has determined that the task, assignment, job, or commission is not to your advantage? You don't. You find and articulate the *business reason* why your serving on this task force, or taking these notes, or writing this report would be a bad idea. You make the case that you can render greater advantage doing something else, or you hint that you might not be right for this assignment, which wouldn't be at all good for the individual trying to stick you with it.

In other words, you don't approach the person handing out the assignment with "I don't think I'm right for this job," or "Isn't there somebody better equipped?" No. You're right for any job, equipped for any task. Rather, suggest the following: "Given the priorities in the department, I wonder if the product management task isn't more pressing than this year-long feasibility study." Remind the boss of your particular strengths, which, you suggest, might be wasted on this particular assignment: "Given my marketing background, do you think I might add greater value on the M&A task force rather than on the Employee Benefits Intranet Committee which really requires more of a technology focus?"

Assuming responsibility that no one else wants to undertake is another by-product of the nurture trap—one to which women are particularly prone. If there's a job that needs to be done, women tend to do it. Why not? It's a perfectly natural train of thought: Somebody has to do this job, and nobody else will, so why shouldn't I?

SCENARIO:

The CFO had called a special meeting regarding the company's investment decisions in the employee defined-contribution plan. It was his meeting with his committee, but several others were there as invited guests to hear the plan and to offer input. Jane, the SVP of human resources, was a member of the committee and attended the meeting along with her staff person, a vice president. As soon as all were seated, Jane looked around the room, saw only other SVPs, turned to the CFO, a colleague, and asked who was taking notes. "Oh," the CFO said, "I don't do notes." Reading his look as meaning that it was her responsibility to do something about the fact that he didn't "do" notes, Jane directed her VP to take notes.

She felt instantly that it had been a mistake to take that responsibility upon her department. She knew the subject matter required minutes for audit purposes; with a staff person at hand, she had the resource to satisfy that need. Yet she always regretted asking the CFO that critical question, "Who's taking notes?" After all, it was the CFO's meeting and the CFO's responsibility, not Jane's. It was just a natural instinct—you see the need and you question how the job was to get done—but it effectively demoted both her department and herself down a notch, and it gave the CFO a power over her he didn't really possess.

Jane's case is not atypical: A perfectly natural, normal behavioral instinct types (or stereotypes) the woman from the start, locking her into an image she has no intention of conveying—an image in the eye of the beholder and therefore, as in Jane's situation, an image she could only control by betraying her natural instinct altogether.

Step 3: Grab—or Create—the Opportunity. Your ten-point checklist has determined that this is a task, job, assignment, or commission you should definitely undertake. To volunteer for it, don't wait for the moment of truth when the boss asks people to raise their hands. It could be too late.

Lay the groundwork first. Make an appointment with *your* boss, whether he's the founder of the assignment or not. Let him know you think you could add value to the corporate task force on changing demographics in the clerical population. Offer reasons. Hint that your value-adding participation could reflect some glory on the boss as well. Then ask for his help.

But don't wait for the task force to be formed, or for the commission to be established, or for the assignment to be devised. Create your own opportunities. The middle manager in financial control who brought her boss a new blueprint for internal operating risk controls and asked to "investigate it further" . . . the woman in IT who suggested to the communications department a contest for coming up with a newsletter title, then designed the contest . . . the sales rep who thought up a strategy for targeting Silicon Valley mergers and acquisitions activity and "gave" it to her boss . . . all these women made extra work for themselves—but made it count.

You can start creating assignments that count now. Fill out a worksheet like the one shown in Figure 8.1 to create a plan for obtaining the significant assignments.

Sometimes, there's a risk involved, as you stick your head out of the comforting carapace of your job description and try to grab something significant. But as the saying goes, never taking a risk is the riskiest thing you can do. And only by doing or creating significant work can women break the mold of being nurturers who can always be counted on for the grunt work.

GETTING TO THE SIGNIFICANT: TEN TIPS

1. Who are the heirs apparent in the organization? What are their interests? Gravitate there. *Better a menial task for the prince than a great big job for a mere pretender.*

2. Got an idea that could be turned into a significant task, study, assignment, even job? *The trick is to frame it right: Show the boss how it can impact the business and make him or her a star.*

3. Take an assignment for strategic reasons—and *only* for strategic reasons. *Define where this project can go and then help to make it get there.*

150

Figure 8.1 A Plan for Obtaining Three Key Assignments.

What are three key assignments I would like to have?

Assignment #1

Assignment #2

Assignment #3

What would I propose to someone in charge of the area the assignment affects—
that is, my idea about the assignment and the contribution I believe the
assignment could make?

Assignment #1

Assignment #2

Assignment #3

Which assignment should I propose first—that is, which is best for me and has
the best chance of being accepted?

What are the key persuasive points to emphasize in the proposal?

Point #1

Point #2

Point #3

When shall I submit my proposal to the appropriate person? _____

4. Avoid the "female ghettoes"—HR, PR, etcetera—and traditional "women's work"—planning the Christmas party, decorating the boss's office—unless there's a solid payback agreed upon up front or the organization truly values these functions and regards those who perform them as business partners with the line managers. *Be seen as a business partner.*

5. Make sure the assignment is viewed by all as a major undertaking and something credited to you. *Take credit and let others give you credit.*

6. Take the risk and grab for the next choice assignment. *If it fits the significant criteria checklist—go for it. Step out of your comfort zone.*

7. Don't have broad shoulders. *Saying "no" builds respect.*

8. Time is something you cannot replace. *Focus your time on the important tasks that will get you a seat of power.*

9. Delegate, follow up, and support your people and others, but don't do their jobs. *The devil may be in the details, but focus on the details in the big picture.*

10. You are better than 90 percent of the people around you including the men. *Act with confidence, take the credit, and stop trying to get it perfect!*

Focus: Do the 80-20 Split

Bill: Women often try to manage too many details on their jobs and fail to focus on the big picture—their careers.

Janice: Well, Bill, if they didn't, there might not be as many results in corporate America, since women seem to do most of the work.

Bill: We won't debate that here, but the point is that in working so hard, women tend to lose sight of where it's getting them.

Janice: We've not only allowed men to delegate the details to us, we've also taken them on. We still seem to have to prove that we can do it all, which we can't, in the hope that we'll win men's approval and get ahead.

Bill: Well, that's not what gets a man's attention, much less his approval. Women have to keep their eyes on the prize, their own personal career objectives. A career is a continuum; you have to pay attention to it on a continual basis. It's a lesson women ignore at their peril.

Janice: Without sacrificing valuable female qualities, women should follow the male model: Delegate more and spend time focusing on "my" career.

"**W**omen are overachievers," says Christina Gold, today a CEO and Vice Chairman of a major telecommunications company. "And women of my generation, the first set of baby boomers, felt it was a privilege to have a seat at the corporate table. It was as if we didn't really have the right to be there, but the guys were nice enough to let us in. I think it's why at first I didn't really focus on career management. I focused instead on delivering the goods and doing the job. I simply didn't take the time to develop the networks and alliances— or to develop myself."

CONSCIENTIOUS OR NAIVE?

Why this single-minded concentration on performance? Is it inherently female to be conscientious—an instinctively maternal tendency to keep all the little ducks in a row and ensure that the "household" is functioning smoothly? Is it cultural—the outsider trying hard to prove herself in an alien world, like the immigrant who works two jobs a day, and menial jobs at that, to secure a beachhead in his new nation's economy? Or is it simply naive—what Carol Taber, former EVP/Group Publisher at Lang Communications, called "the classic belief that if you work hard you'd get patted on the head and get rewarded"?

Whatever the reason, the single-mindedness of women's concentration on their current job assignment has time and again proven to be self-defeating. As Taber points out, while she looked forward to being rewarded for being "dedicated and loyal and hardworking . . . the guy in the next office was off playing tennis with the chairman." As she said, "I was killing myself to excel and yet around me was all this mediocrity."

Even then, Taber admits she didn't get it. "I can remember a guy saying to me after I had whipped the department into shape that I was 'herculean.' He was amazed. 'You are herculean,' he told me, 'I'm just a man.' I thought I had been pretty herculean too, and I thought I should be promoted. So I approached my boss and said that with several people retiring, maybe I would have an opportunity to have one of those positions. My boss said that would come in time." The position no doubt went instead to the guy playing tennis with the chairman.

Unfair? Without question. But fairness is not the issue. Power is the issue.

"Meritocracy does not always exist in corporate America," says Marilyn Puder-York. Taber agrees. "Meritocracy stops working" at the higher levels of the organization. "There are stories upon stories of women who on their merits should have risen," Taber asserts. "But these women tend to assume they will get noticed. They will not." Something more is needed, something beyond merit, performance, herculean effort, and stellar results.

What is needed is a focus on career and on doing what we call the 80-20 split.

BALANCING ACT

This does not mean putting politics before performance. Fudging your way upward on charm and Machiavellian machinations alone probably never worked—unless you were the chairman's nephew. It certainly does not work in today's sleeker, downsized corporations in which an individual corporate officer's job may comprise the responsibilities once executed by two or three or even more people.

Of course, you must concentrate on the job; without the job, there is no career path at all. But you must concentrate on the job within the wider context of the career and your personal goals for the career. In the often dog-eat-dog world of today's corporate politics, you can't afford not to keep an eye on the road up ahead. At the same time, you can't afford not to keep an eye on your current assignment, especially since in today's sleeker, downsized corporations, failures are easily spotted and little tolerated.

But of course, keeping one eye on today and one on tomorrow can make a person cross-eyed. Carole Taber uses a different metaphor. "It really is a delicate dance," Taber says, "in which you have to be focused on wanting to get to the top, while achieving the excellence in your current position that can leverage you to that goal."

How should you choreograph the dance to achieve the right balance? Do the 80-20 split. That is, spend 80 percent of your time doing your job and achieving performance. Spend 20 percent of your time on the equally important assignment of managing your career to achieve the personal fulfillment and success you want in life.

THE 80-20 SPLIT

Yes, we can hear your panicked peals of hysterical laughter. Do the job in only 80 percent of my time? you ask. I can barely do it in 150 percent of the time! We believe you, but the question is: What are you going to do about it?

Actually, the idea that the job is simply too big to get done is not just a cliché, it is also one of the great canards of corporate life. The old knife-twisting crack—"Half-day today?"—when you are staggering out the door at 11 p.m. for the fifth time this week is by now something of a "gotcha," a gloater's trump card that is just so much hooey. Hours logged in the office may be a litmus test of how much you want to impress the boss, or of a culture of paranoia, but they don't tell much about how effective you are. In fact, spending too much time getting the job done can actually be self-defeating, if not downright self-destructive.

Come on, 'fess up. Do you really have to put in all those hours? Most late workers are addicted to not leaving the office. They feel more comfortable there than at home. Is that you?

SCENARIO:

With her background as an officer in the Navy and her training as an electrical engineer, Margaret W. quickly gained a reputation as an exceptionally thorough and effective manager. She approached every project as a military exercise, every problem as a war to be won. Then she attacked—and invariably succeeded. At the heart of her success was attention to detail, a personality trait honed to a fine art in the Navy, where, as Margaret said, "failure to control even the smallest detail could mean the difference between life and death." Although her staff was highly qualified and effective, and although she trusted them all, Margaret always insisted on "one last look, one final check." As her reputation for "cleaning up messes" grew, she was assigned to more and more of them. "Captain Turnaround," they called her, but with all her time spent on the job at hand, and with more and more people relying on her to serve as a one-woman swat team, Margaret was increasingly locked into her reputation. Her own single-mindedness about "doing the job assigned" and her very success at the job made it likely that she'd be Captain Turnaround forever—when what she really wanted was to be Admiral of an entire fleet.

One moral of Margaret's story is that if you do something very very well, you may get stuck doing it forever. And with her own insistence on doing every final check herself, she isn't leaving herself any time to broaden or enrich her reputation, do the bonding and alliance-building she needs to, or create the networks and power bases she requires. All she has going for her is talent and performance, and while they are essential, even both of them together, however exceptional, are not enough to raise you to the rank of Admiral. Nor should they be.

FIVE STEPS

In fact, by the time you've reached the director or vice president level, your job is really two jobs. Job One is the corporate function for which you've been given responsibility. Job Two is the management of your own career. Together, they should take 100 percent of your professional time—80 percent for the current corporate function, 20 percent for the long-range career design. In today's world, in fact, with corporate loyalty going the way of the dinosaur, it may be more realistic to think about a 75-25 split—even 60-40. But for conceptual purposes, start with 80-20.

Here's how to make the split.

Step 1: Identify the 80. The best way to carry out your corporate job function in 80 percent of your time is to delegate a significant portion of the job's responsibilities to staff. How much? We estimate a third. Which third? The least visible.

Figuring out what's visible and what's invisible is easier than it sounds, and we've designed a form to make it even easier, the visibility meter, shown in Figure 9.1.

Start with your job description, performance review, or annual objectives—whatever it is that lists your responsibilities and the objectives for each area of responsibility. Go down the list of tasks and, one by one, ask yourself the following questions:

1. Is the work visible in the corporation?
2. Does the work have an impact?
3. Is the task sensitive—that is, does it involve confidential information or touch on strategic planning or the like?
4. Will this responsibility lead to innovation?
5. Could it blow the place up?
6. Is it long-term?
7. Will it have an immediate, direct effect on earnings?

By now you've figured out where we're going with this because the keywords spell it out: Is the task **visible?** Will executing the responsibility make *you* visible? If it meets any of these criteria, it is and it will. Keep it. All other tasks and responsibilities: Delegate!

Step 2: Do or Delegate. For example, you may be in charge of your company's communications policy. In that capacity, you determine who

Figure 9.1 Visibility Meter.

Responsibility/ Function/ Task	visible?	impact?	sensitive?	innovation?	blow up?	long-term?	effect on earnings?
1.							
2.							
3.							
4.							
5.							
6.							

Jot down the key responsibility, function, or task. Then go across each column and answer honestly if the work meets the criteria of visibility. Unless you can answer YES, it's work you shouldn't be doing.

will be a spokesman for the company. You also approve every press release. You set the strategy for the company's communications piece, but you do not do the company newsletter: Delegate it.

You always want to control the follow-up on something like a due diligence process for a proposed acquisition, but not the follow-up on an action plan for the next off-site conference. Keep the former, delegate the latter.

And while you must keep in your hands the development and execution of the company's brand identity strategy, you don't need to monitor every market research study on client response to every slogan, ad, or product innovation. Delegate the monitoring; the research results are review items that can be assessed as part of the normal weekly or monthly review agenda.

Even in a crisis, it pays to delegate—as long as you establish a clear process and set hard-and-fast ground rules up front about exactly what you need to know and exactly when you need to know it. In fact, whether managing a crisis or the day-to-day work, it makes sense to lay out a clear delegation of responsibility procedure, showing who is responsible for which actions, who has approval/veto authority, and

Figure 9.2 Delegation of Responsibility.

Action to be taken	Who is responsible for action?	Who has veto/approval?	Who has to be informed?	Who needs to provide resources/support?

who has to be kept informed. Chart the procedure, as in the worksheet in Figure 9.2.

Do the visible and control it, delegate what's not visible and follow up regularly on what you delegate—after all, it might become visible at any moment—and you can easily do 100 percent of the job assigned to you in 80 percent of your time.

Step 3: Manage Your Career 20 Percent of the Time. The other 20 percent of your time should be dedicated to Job Two, a job that is critical to your key business . . . your career. Create a special workspace for this job—a special file folder on the computer, a distinct set of schedules on your handheld, a separate shortcut on your personal information manager.

What should fill this workspace? You will find the answers in a monthly task and a semiannual exercise.

THE MONTHLY QUESTIONNAIRE

The monthly task consists of asking yourself five key questions, answering them honestly, and taking action on the answers. Preferably at the end of the workday on the last Friday of the month, perhaps on the train commute home, or in some situation in which you will not be interrupted, define your month-end by asking yourself these questions:

1. Did I gain information about the company and its business? This can include any and every kind of knowledge: technical information, a deeper understanding of world economic events, learning a new fact about the company—whatever you learned that you might conceivably use some day.

2. Did I add a skill to my portfolio? Again, the aim is to have picked up a skill that can be applied to improve the business, build your reputation, and thus advance your own agenda.

3. Did I advance my network? You advance your network by adding to alliances or strengthening existing alliances. Determine whether you did either of those.

4. What did I do to increase my fan club? Your fan club comprises those peers, subordinates, even superiors who think you're great. One or some of them need to be contacted, nurtured, supported each month. Who was it this month? What happened?

5. Did I advance my career strategy to get where I want to be when I want to get there—or not?

Where the answer to a question is yes, make note of it so you can enhance the advance—that is, use what was learned; polish the skill; bolster the alliance; strengthen the bond of loyalty; move forward on the strategy.

Where the answer is no, develop an action plan. Initiate it the following day, so that by next month's interrogation, you will have changed the no answer to yes.

Step 4: The Semiannual Review. In addition to the monthly exam, carve out a block of time twice a year to anticipate the unknown. What are the signals within the corporation and in the wider economy to which you should be alert? Take their pulse twice a year, then create what-if scenarios that focus on you and your career.

For example, what if the chairman/CEO suddenly retires? What will happen to you? Will it be good or bad for your career if the current second-in-command takes over? Or is another person gaining popularity and therefore a likely successor to the CEO? In any scenario, what must you do to make sure it's good for you?

Or what if the company is bought? Where do you stand? Do you have a retention agreement? Would your pension and stock options be protected? How long a grace period might be given? Would you be eligible for that protection? If not, do you have the leverage to become eligible? If not, how can you get it?

What if the corporation's stock price suddenly takes a dive? What if it soars? What might be the effect on your boss, your department, your job?

To meet these what-if scenarios, develop contingency action plans. You may never need any of them, but simply going through the exercise of the supposing, the answering, and the strategic thinking will clarify the context of your own career and advance your skills for managing your individual career plan. You'll find you're better positioned to identify opportunities when they arise—and to seize the moment.

THE CORPORATE LIFE EQUATION:
80 + 20 = 100

We typically get a funny reaction when we tell a roomful of corporate women that "your career is what takes you through life." We get booed and cheered at the same time—sometimes simultaneously by a single individual.

It's not particularly surprising. Women have been conditioned to believe that what they should really value in life is children, spouse, the murmurs of the heart. Of course, that's true. But it's equally true that children grow up and leave, that a husband or partner is a companion and lover and not a purpose in life, and that the heart is strongest when it's being put to good use.

Study after study shows that what people really want in life is to make an impact . . . to contribute their skills, knowledge, and abilities and make a difference. A career can do that for you. It's a vehicle of self-fulfillment. It can take care of your need to leave an impression that bears your unique signature. But you have to take care of the career, too. It's your job—as much as carrying out your corporate responsibility.

And it really is a job only you can do.

Power: Be a General by Being a Generalist

Bill: The buzzword in skill requirements today is to be "multi-specialized."

Janice: That is key to general management. After a couple of decades of filling ranks with technical specialties, corporations are once again competing for general managers, people who know how to run businesses. The trick is that to run businesses today, you are better prepared if you are a multi-specialist, someone who understands the overall operations of the business, particularly from a technology perspective.

Bill: The trick is to find business leaders who understand the technical aspects of the business and have the people skills and managerial know-how to put it all together.

Janice: All businesses—the dot-coms, the new economy start-ups, and the old economy Fortune 500—are finding that the one quality they absolutely cannot do without is the quintessential general management skill. The need is so great that gender issues should not be an issue.

Bill: You're absolutely right on—a great opportunity for women to seize!

Professional development. It's one area in which men are almost as badly off as women. The needs of twenty-first century business seem to have caught corporate management unawares, so that management now finds itself unprepared, ill-equipped, and with its proverbial pants down around its proverbial ankles. For women, the urgent need for managerial leadership can be an opportunity.

Why is the need so great? For a couple of decades at least, as they confronted the escalating competitive pressures of the global economy, American corporations laid off hundreds of thousands of middle managers who were developing generalist skills. They recruited technical skills as fast as they could find them. Technology specialists to deploy within the computing and telecommunications infrastructure. Operations research types to re-engineer business processes. Financial whiz kids to handle the due diligence on mergers and acquisitions.

But at the end of the day, when corporate management looked up from its headlong rush to restructure and downsize, there was one big, gaping hole in the professional ranks: generalists who could manage the technical specialists and capitalize on their strengths to implement and successfully realize a corporate strategy. Of course, there were some "natural" managers among the technocrats hired in the latter part of the twentieth century, but not enough. People born with the talent to manage are few and far between. Instead, general managers need to be developed—that is, given the training and the experience and skills that will be needed to manage the twenty-first-century corporation.

The problem is that the training, experience, and skills needed to be a general manager today are so far beyond anything that has ever been required before that corporations themselves are at a loss how to make good generalist managers. One thing is certain: Versatility is only a beginning.

MULTISPECIALIZING

What are the skills and competencies a manager needs today? Begin with complete familiarity with the basic functions of any business: finance, marketing, sales, operations, human resources, strategic planning, risk management. Equally basic today are computer skills, Internet awareness, and familiarity with e-commerce. You've also got to have line P&L experience, motivation skills, communication skills, hands-on digital expertise. It helps to have managed change, slashed expenses, written a winning proposal, mentored or coached. You'd better know the law in such areas as employee relations, sexual harassment, global trade, and the worldwide regulatory environment. Can you manage your time? Delegate? Motivate? Give and receive feedback? Set goals? Inspire the troops? Remember everybody's name? The list goes on and on, yet that's what basic management requires in the twenty-first century.

It's a formidable list of requirements. As curriculums go, the multispecialist's checklist is a demanding one. Think of it as a pyramid, as shown in Figure 10.1. The foundation underlying everything else is built of the basic competencies of any good business manager. In the mid-range is the expertise that is particularly germane to the organization—the skills required to realize the particular purpose of a company, whatever its industry, whatever it is selling. At the apex are the general management skills that can make a synergy of the basic competencies and the company-specific specialties, the generalist qualities that can bring all the resources of the organization together to drive it toward its purpose.

How well prepared are you to climb up the pyramid? How close are you to becoming a multispecialist, the kind of generalist who's becoming the general these days? To find out, fill out a preparedness list worksheet like the one in Figure 10.2. Don't be too hard on yourself—everybody has blind spots, deficiencies, gaps in their learning—but do be honest.

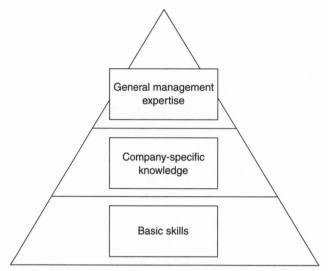

Figure 10.1 The Multispecialist's Pyramid.

LEVEL PLAYING FIELD = HIGH OPPORTUNITY

The war for talent—the simple law of supply and demand—has leveled the playing field for men and women. Two factors are keeping it flat.

First, the multispecialist curriculum. It's a lot to learn, it's difficult material, and much of it is brand-new stuff. Second, professional development programs in American corporations, despite a lot of talk, are both poorly designed to meet specific company and individual needs and ineffectively administered.

Add up these two realities and the bottom line is that men and women are really at a similar starting point when it comes to having a chance at general management.

We've talked about the multispecialist curriculum. Professional development programs, you would think, would address that curriculum so as to prepare today's corporate managers for tomorrow's challenges. But professional development programs are one of the saddest stories in corporate America. Honored far more in theory than in fact, given more lip service than resources, they represent a

Figure 10.2 Multispecialist's Preparedness List.

Basic Skills	Y/N	Company-Specific Knowledge	Y/N	General Management Expertise	Y/N
Written communications		Balance sheet		Management of people	
Technology proficiency		P&L		Developing executive business plan	
Finance		Public relations posture		International experience	
Marketing		Annual reports		Strategy management	
Presentations		Analysts' reports		Visionary leadership	
Interpersonal		Accounting		Excellent communicator	
Running meetings		M&A		Understands importance of technology to business	
Business planning		Divestitures		Goal-setting (one month to ten years)	
Managing people		Competitive arena		Budget management	

considerable lost opportunity. An organization might offer a training session every six months—with no continuity maintaining the learning from one session to the next. Or senior management will send the hottest rainmaker off for "leadership development" training, when his inclination and his best use are to keep on doing deals, not to lead people. A mistake. Some people are best left to do what they do best.

The upshot for women is that the level playing field offers them a fertile opportunity to gain an important foothold on the future of corporate America, but the formal channels of development are either dried up or nonexistent. The solution? Self-administered professional development. Here is a chance for women to invest in themselves and in their own education—and potentially reap the leadership of tomorrow's executive suite.

How to do it? Think volleyball: Rotate.

THE ROTATION PRINCIPLE

Job rotation is a time-honored prescription for professional development, but it has typically been reserved for the young lions of the company. Locked in the vault of every HR department in corporate America is the fast-tracker file, the HiPo (high-potential) list, the book of "Corporate Assets"—that is, the rising stars the corporation wants to groom for leadership, the people they want to keep happy and well compensated and moving ahead, the anointed princes or princesses marked for ownership of the company's future. For such people, professional development plans are drawn up, reviewed, reassessed, and tweaked at least once a year, if not more often—typically by a select committee of high-level corporate management. Outside executive coaches are often engaged to beef up the fast-track team of executives. At the heart of these development plans is the simple notion of job rotation: moving the fast-trackers from one core function to another, one professional discipline to another, one kind of challenge to another. It's a process of education aimed at breeding generalists. It's a planned progression through experience. It's also a weeding-out process: Some of the HiPos will fail, but those who succeed will have become precisely the all-around leaders the corporation is looking for.

THREE STEPS

Our strategic recommendation for multispecializing is to create your own rotation plan, your own personal plan of professional development. Here's a three-step approach for doing so.

Step 1: Lock in the Basics. If you're lacking in the basics, now's the time to rectify the situation. Finance, marketing, sales, operations, human resources, strategic planning, risk management: If you're weak in any one of these areas, plug the hole by taking a course, attending a workshop, reading a book, or talking to specialists in your company or outside the organization.

A mid-level marketing manager we know—a woman who had worked her way up from secretary and had no formal business training—quickly realized that her financial skills were nil. At her own expense, she hired a financial consultant to put her through one-on-one training until she felt fully confident of her financial abilities and fully versed in the subject matter. (In fact, her new reputation as a source of financial understanding prompted her to "share" the consultant with colleagues in marketing, operations, and sales. That, in turn, earned her a quid pro quo to be repaid later, and it solidified her reputation as an imaginative go-getter. A winning proposition all around.)

So the first necessity is to do whatever it takes to put yourself through business school—either literally or figuratively. Start with a needs assessment, a good way to lock in the basics. A worksheet like the one in Figure 10.3 will help you prepare for the moment when opportunity knocks.

Figure 10.3 Needs Assessment: Locking in the Basics.

What are the basics I need to learn?	How will I learn them?	Timetable

Step 2: Specialize in Your Company's Driving Forces. What drives your organization? Whatever it is, certain skills and disciplines are pertinent to the drivers, and those are the competencies in which you must specialize.

Go back to the worksheet you created for Strategy 2 on fitting in to again take the temperature of your organization. What are the skills that define its type, describe its leadership and operating style, give it a personality? What are the competencies that shape your company's culture? Find them, and then make yourself an expert in them. Use a worksheet like the one shown in Figure 10.4 to remind yourself of the driving forces in your organization.

Is yours an analytical corporation? Brush up on your financial skills, even if your job is in marketing. Make sure you know which divisions are growing and making money for the company—and which are not. Get access to the monthly numbers of the organization, and learn them cold—whether it's your job to know them or not.

Or perhaps your company is an innovative organization in which out-of-the-box thinking is prized. Your job, however, is to manage a day-to-day operation that seems never to change. It's a perfect perch from which to make yourself an expert on the latest thinking in the field. Keep up with the state of the art in technology. Subscribe to the farthest-out of the far-out business publications. It may not be possible to learn imaginative thinking, but it is eminently possible to become an expert in the innovations being discussed in the business world at large and in your industry in particular.

Figure 10.4 Driving Forces in My Organization.

What are the drivers in the organization?	Who are the drivers?	How do I become a driver or get with the driver?

Step 3: Create Your Own Generalist Development Plan. The fact that many companies do not follow through on professional development

programs doesn't mean the programs aren't in place. They are. Use them. Career planning, performance coaching, and a raft of training courses are the usual substance of the typical corporate offering for professional development. Take advantage of the offering—even if you're the only one—and push your boss to sign you up.

But be sure to broadcast the fact that you're signing up. Let it be known that you're interested in developing your potential—and that you're working at it. When you have your performance review, discuss the issue with your boss. Ask him what he recommends for you, and ascertain what time and resources he might allow you for development training. Know what's available, and be persuasive about how you think it can help you help the business. And if the boss suggests that you need to work on a few skills, ask him for the resources to go to school and get them.

If the in-house offering isn't sufficient or pertinent, go outside for what you need. Do it at your own expense if you must, but then make sure that the boss knows you've done so. Let him know, too, if you've found something useful externally that might be imported to become a part of the in-house curriculum. Talk about it with other wannabes and start a groundswell movement for meeting development needs in the organization.

One more thing: If the boss says no to your development plan once, you can always try again. If he says no at the next performance review as well, that's perhaps understandable; after all, he probably has a lot on his plate and can't afford right now to let you spend time advancing your own learning process. But if you're rejected time and again, perhaps the company is not willing to invest in you and your future. Perhaps you are not considered a HiPo or an asset or the kind of manager this company wants. That sounds like a signal to get out of the company, a hint that you're in the wrong organization. Go somewhere where your talents and qualifications are sufficiently regarded, where the organization is willing to invest resources in turning you into the general manager it ought to know it needs.

WHEN AND HOW

You mean you don't have a development plan? Don't feel too bad. Ninety percent of the women we interviewed for this book didn't have one either. Still, it's important to draw one up. Like New Year's resolutions, unless you put a personal professional development plan on paper and post it on the refrigerator door, you're not really paying attention.

When should you draw up a plan? Now. The sooner the better. It's a plan that will evolve continually over time as you add new experiences to your background and learn additional skills. But the plan should begin when the career does.

Figure 10.5 shows a worksheet for creating your personal professional development plan. Go back to the preparedness list you prepared earlier—like the one in Figure 10.2 on page 169—and check off the skills or competencies you lack or in which you feel weak. Transfer those learning needs to the worksheet, and define a plan for doing whatever is needed to fill the gap.

That might mean finding a course you can take during the evenings or on weekends. Self-study has become increasingly feasible with the growth of the Internet. Now, you can take a course at your convenience. You can also participate in online sessions with experts—albeit at their convenience.

Devising your plan might mean gaining a particular experience—and if so, you'll need to plot how to get a particular assignment. It might mean "apprenticing" yourself to an expert in the organization; again, you will need to arrange the assignment in some way.

Whatever will get you across the delta between what you know and what you need to know is another step toward general manage-

Figure 10.5 My Personal Professional Development Plan.

Key Learning Needs	Status	How to Obtain Internally	External Sources
	Have/Need	Tasks/Programs/ People	Tasks/Programs/ People
Basic skills 1 2 3			
Company-specific knowledge 1 2 3			
General management expertise 1 2 3			

ment multispecialization—and thus toward the possibility of leadership in the corporation.

Eight tips for multispecializing to become a generalist

1. Look for opportunities to help colleagues in a driving unit of the organization—or in a unit that needs development. They may return the favor later and you'll learn from that experience.

2. Industry associations and such generalist organizations as The Conference Board constantly offer training, workshops, and seminars. Check their course lists for items that match your personal checklist.

3. Become a student for the rest of your life. Books, tapes, journals, networks, and professional groups offer a variety of learning opportunities.

4. Figure out the two key skills the company values that are different from your own area of expertise and focus on developing them. If one of the two skills the organization prizes most is a skill you already possess, become the known in-house expert; even so, add one more skill to your arsenal.

5. Learn about other areas of the organization through the people who do the work. People in the lower rungs of the corporation are happy to talk about what they do, so visit other departments and ask them. It's a good way to learn a function.

6. In meetings, let people know you want to learn about their area of the business. Ask questions; offer solutions.

7. Make your development plan an agenda item during performance review discussions.

8. Take a lateral move and do a job rotation.

....

Sex: Take It
or Leave It,
but Control It

Janice: Bill, did you ever have an office romance?

Bill: Yes, it was a disaster. Did you, Janice?

Janice: Yes. I married him.

From disaster to marriage and everywhere in between, sex exists in corporate America. This is not exactly a revelation of the man-bites-dog variety. There's sex in every workplace. Assembly line or executive suite, farm field or groves of academe, wherever and whenever men and women are together, sharing tasks and a purpose and depending on one another to get the tasks done, this most elemental fact of life will inevitably kick in.

USA Today reported several years ago that women prefer to meet men at the office. Of course. It beats being "hit on" at a bar, and it's far more telling than meeting someone at a party or through a fix-up. After all, work with someone eight hours a day, day after day, and you get to know him pretty well. You see how he acts, how he reacts under pressure, how he interacts with and manages people, how he thinks, what he values, his sense of humor—if he has one. If you work together, you already share a third of your lives—the work third—so the distance to sharing the rest is not very great.

And that is why love is so quick to bloom in the garden of corporate America. Walt Wriston, onetime CEO of what was then Citicorp, told a group of employees about the day the institution struck down the rule that had prohibited any two people of vice presidential level or above from being married to one another. The minute the rule change was published, Wriston recalled, the married senior managers "started coming out of the woodwork," relieved that they no longer had to keep their marriages a secret.

SCENARIO:

An off-site meeting of the senior team was capped by a late night of socializing, including drinking and dancing. When the festivities finally wound down, a certain male executive approached Margaret, a senior vice president with a clear shot at a managing director title, and offered to walk her back to her room in the hotel. Not wanting to appear ungrateful, she agreed. When they arrived at her door, it quickly became clear that he was waiting to be invited in. It was a situation requiring both sensitivity and skill, and she brought both to bear. "I know you and I know your wife," she said, "and I have such a respect for you that I'm just going to say good night." The spurned executive, however, disliked any type of rejection, and he never forgot this one. The MD slot reported to him, and when the expected opening occurred, and the departing managing director recommended Margaret as his successor—"the best qualified person for the job," he said—the position nevertheless went to an older man who had already announced his retirement. Cause and effect? A bruised male ego unable to allow a rejecting female a choice position reporting to him? Such things are hard to prove, but Margaret was in no doubt as to the cause. She left the corporation a year later to get the title and position she deserved elsewhere—without the encumbering entanglements sex too often intrudes into the process.

The lesson? It can be dangerous for women and men to mix business and pleasure—even when doing the right thing. From the start, expectations make this a very volatile combination. Women— particularly single younger women—tend to see office relationships in terms of romantic potential. Men and some married women see them as short-term escapes—often from unhappy marriages, pressure-packed jobs, or unfulfilling sex lives. So if you're thinking about having an affair with someone in the office, the chances are high from the start that you and your potential partner(s) will have different expectations for the outcome of the affair.

THE FACTS OF LIFE ABOUT THE FACTS OF LIFE IN THE OFFICE

We debated whether to even include this topic in our book. It's so personal, so dependent on individual situations. Besides, we presume that everyone reading this book is an adult who will consent or not according to her own principles, values, and desires. But what we heard from women of all ages and at all stages of the corporate career convinced us that the issue of sex at the office is as prevalent as ever. Even the dot-coms have resorted to hiring HR directors to stay out of the courts, since what they think of as their easygoing cultures increasingly gives rise to harassment charges.

Our view is that, except for instances of coercion or other forms of harassment, whatever goes on between adult men and women in the corporate world is their business and nobody else's—as long as it doesn't affect their jobs or the jobs of those around them.

Unfortunately, it doesn't always work out that way. On the contrary. The fact is that office romances rarely work out at all—especially in the fairly rarefied atmosphere of senior management, where "having a job" is equivalent to holding a highly visible position of leadership and authority. From our research and our collective experience as managers, coaches, and recruiters, *at least* 90 percent of office relationships we know about have failed. And while both parties to such a romance may suffer the hurt that the end of an affair always brings, it

179

is the woman who typically suffers the most. Not only will she face the emotional distress that people typically suffer at a break-up, she may also sustain a swift kick right in the career.

It is true that times have changed. It is increasingly the case that men, too, are finding sex at the office to be dangerous turf. But times have not changed all that much or all that fast. For the foreseeable future, it is still the woman who runs the risk of a dead-ended career for the sake of sex. What's more, it is the woman who will be damned if she does, damned if she doesn't—stopped in her upward track because she's more known for her love affair than for her management skills, or isolated out on a narrow limb because her "no" stirred the ire of a rejected suitor.

On the other hand, how many snide stories do you hear about men sleeping their way to the top of the corporation? And how many male executives find their careers jeopardized because they have a reputation as a ladies' man? A double standard? You bet. Where sex in the corporate office is concerned, it remains a man's world. Although damaged, unless his actions make the far right column in the *Wall Street Journal*, the majority of the time a man will walk away from the liaison in better career shape than a woman.

So the overriding lesson about sex in the office is that it does carry a price tag and that, nine times out of ten, it is the woman who pays. There is thus a simple strategy for sex relationships at the office: Avoid them if you can. And, if one or both of you are married, really avoid any relationship.

THREE STEPS

There are two sex-at-the-office situations requiring strategic action. One is when you find yourself attracted to, romantically inclined toward, or in love with someone you work with. The other is when sex at the office is a problem. Maybe it's an unwanted but persistent advance directed toward you. Maybe you're aware of a situation of sexual harassment. Maybe someone else's affair is blatantly getting in the way of getting work done, is leading to decisions based on something other than good business sense, or is responsible for the promotion of someone who doesn't deserve it in favor of someone who does—like maybe you. You may be the boss of someone involved in what you consider a dubious romantic proposition; you may be reporting to someone having an affair with "the wrong person." In other words, you can be impacted by an office romance even when it's somebody else's romance. (Talk about having all of the pain and none of the pleasure!)

Both sets of situations prove the rule: Sex doesn't belong at the office.

But, of course, if it were possible to avoid sex at the office simply by snapping your fingers, we wouldn't need a chapter on the subject in this book. The whole point about what goes on between two people is what it does to good sense. Recent research has confirmed scientifically what everyone has known since the beginning of time: Love muddles the brain, actually altering its chemistry. Objective thinking goes right out the window. In the excitement of it all, the importance of today's objectives becomes a joke, while long-term career goals toward which you've struggled can seem paltry. You cease to care about those things any more. You're blinded by love. Or are you?

Of course not. You're an adult, with the power to control your actions. Yes, you're distracted by this attraction, and no, you're not thinking clearly. But you haven't given up the inherent ability to think and act. An approach for dealing with sex at the office is based in that fundamental premise.

Step 1: Count the Cost. Let's start with the first situation: You're attracted, distracted, and impacted just about every minute of the day. Still, you have not lost all reason, all power, all self-control. You're still capable of measuring and judging.

So at the very least, look before you leap. Be aware of what it may cost you. That way, if the relationship should fail, you will be prepared to deal with the consequences.

Remind yourself, therefore, of the following:

1. This romance will not conquer all obstacles.

2. My objectivity is already skewed.

3. My job performance will probably be affected.

4. My reputation will certainly be impacted. I may be talked about more for my sex life than for my accomplishments.

5. All relationships are challenging; relationships at work are especially challenging.

We do know of one very well-known and successful business woman who shrewdly manipulated an office romance with her married boss. Using what used to be known as her "feminine wiles," she made sure she got the title, the compensation, the office, and the authority first. Her methodology got her what she wanted from a power and money perspective; it also gained her a reputation for her sexual prowess.

Take note of what you can lose by this office romance: status, face, and eventually, the man, too. Evaluate the downside for your career, a career that will, you hope, take you through life—as opposed to an affair that will probably not last. Weigh the career impact against what you feel to be the inevitability of this affair. If you still think it's worth it, at least you're ready for the pitfalls and prepared to pay the piper.

Step 2: In Love? Keep It Businesslike. There's a good rule of thumb for managing an office romance on the job—yours or anyone else's. It's this: Stick to business. Love is love, and work is work, and never should the twain meet between the moment you enter the office and the moment you leave it at night. What's more, while you and your love are in the office together, any interaction between you should be strictly business, and it should be conducted in a businesslike manner. Even if you're alone together, render respect for the company that's paying you. Behave according to company rules.

Many corporations, in fact, maintain rules on office romance; often, those rules require the parties to disclose their affair. Even if there is no such rule, disclosure is a good idea. That doesn't mean holding a press conference or hiring a brass band to accompany an announcement over the PA system, but it does mean you should let both bosses—yours and his—know that you are dating. If you're in a reporting relationship—whether you report to him or he reports to you—informing the next level up is absolutely essential, even if you're in the first throes of serious dating. This may result in one of you getting transferred, but that's better than jeopardizing your career.

Of course, if you're sticking to the basic rule of thumb, there will be no bragging, no exhibitionism, no details told over the office phone, no lamentations in the ladies' room if and when the affair ends. In short, act like a grown-up. Remain personally respectful of him the whole time you're together, and keep it up afterwards if it doesn't work out. No one wants to hear about the blow-up or about how well it's going. Trust us on this. Only gossips want to hear the details—and they'll probably use the details to do you harm.

Step 3: Deflect the Unwanted Advance. As frequent an occurrence as the mutually sought office romance is the unsought advance. Unsought, unwanted, and unappreciated. Of course, most women have been in training since childhood in how to reject an unwanted advance. The difference is that this is the workplace. This is not a bar or a party or a blind date where a woman can blithely tell a guy to take a hike, with whatever degree of courtesy she feels up to. This is the environment in which the woman is making a career. The guy making the unwanted advance is someone with whom she works, someone she'll see in a meeting tomorrow, will work with the next day, may have working for her the day after or work for next week. It all complicates the issue.

How do you deal with the unwanted advance in the office? Slowly. Carefully. Calmly. Without emotion. In progressive steps.

"There are usually two common situations involving sex in the office," comments psychologist and executive coach, Dr. Marilyn Puder-York. "The first involves a woman who takes a compliment to heart and believes it and acts on it. The second is where men send out very strong messages on a constant basis; it's usually a rather controlling, sadistic guy who, in a very passive-aggressive way, sends out very seductive signals.

"When the woman picks up on the signals, he denies that he ever gave out any signals. However, situations are never this clear. It depends on the persons involved. How does the woman respond? She has to figure out what the reality is. She may be enraged. But maybe she is just having a bad day. She needs to do a reality check. Do not act out your emotions when you're provoked. Think about what provoked you; was it the first time this has happened or is it a pattern? What response did you give, if any? Think about these things before you go and tell others in the company about the situation. And if you are going to confide in human resources or your boss, what are the possible ramifications of that action? It's better to do nothing until your emotions are in check and you have a plan of action."

Let's assume your emotions *are* in check. You've been approached more than once, and more than once you've tried to make it clear that you're not interested in a relationship. He persists. What do you do? Take it one step at a time.

1. The first time it happens, be pleasant, be cool, be firm, and move out of his space. Remember the rule of thumb—stick to business—and make it your mantra. He's being suggestive? Be businesslike. He keeps changing the subject to the idea of having a drink or dinner? Change it back: "How about those monthly

sales figures?" or "What do you think of the new product development plan?" Let him know you're here to work.

2. The second time it happens, use humor. Laugh it off. "I'm flattered, but I bet you say that to all the women." Or "Left your glasses at home?" or "How much did they pay you to say that?" Humor is a great deflector. Wit is a superb weapon for cutting off the unwanted overture. Put him down with humor, and you can actually enhance your reputation.

3. By the third or fourth incident, it's time to send him to the proverbial cold shower. Resort to the dreaded "Let's just be friends." It's about as clear as a rejection can be. Don't be afraid to use it, at any point, if politeness or humor don't work.

4. If he still won't take no for an answer, take action. Unwanted sexual advances that occur more than once can be considered harassment. Report the problem to the ranking officer—in most cases, your boss—who should be attentive to your predicament. An investment banker we know tried all three first steps to no avail. Finally, she went to her boss. He was furious, held the male suitor responsible, and took immediate action. It cost the violator a promotion and a raise. It also very forcefully defined the environment; from now on, everyone knew that such actions had specific consequences.

5. If your boss can't or won't resolve the matter, consult with human resources on the best way to handle the situation. If you register a complaint with your human resources department, it's on the record. So if anyone in the company takes any action against you, it can be seen as retaliation and grounds for a lawsuit.

6. If internal resources fail to resolve the matter, you should talk to a lawyer—preferably one with expertise in sexual harassment cases—about how to proceed.

None of these alternatives is pleasant, of course, and a lot of women we know have had unpleasant experiences trying to deal with harassment issues altogether. One CFO of a major telecommunications firm says, without reserve, that she would never again appeal to the powers-that-be in an organization about unwelcome sexual advances. "Oh goodness, no!" this CFO told us. "I did that once and boy, did it backfire. I was at a dinner with a senior officer in the company and some bankers. The guy made some derogatory comments about why I would never get ahead because I didn't play around. I was so mortified and angry that I ended up going to the office of the general counsel, who was in charge of human resources, to complain about his offensiveness. My guy buddies came to me afterward and said, 'Why did you go and do a thing like that? You know he just drinks and talks too much.' "

This woman says that rather than complain again she would leave the company and go elsewhere. That may not be the right thing to do, but we suspect a lot of women feel the same way. It's an unhappy comment on the entire situation, but it's also a fact of life you need to be aware of.

OFFICE SEX AND THE LAW

SCENARIO:

When the top managers' meeting was held in a district for which she was responsible, Senior Regional Manager Patricia was invited as a matter of course. It turned out, however, that she was the only woman in attendance, and as the evening wore on and the cocktails continued to flow, Patricia grew increasingly uncomfortable. It wasn't just the looks she was getting, it was also the general tone of the conversation, not to mention the tenor of the jokes.

She decided to exit as quickly and gracefully as possible, but first, of course, she needed to pay her respects to the boss. She thanked him for the invitation and extended her hand to shake his. He took her hand, held it, then pulled her toward him and, in plain view of a group of other managers, all male, kissed her on the mouth. Patricia was stunned. So were the managers who had seen the incident. As she turned and walked out the door, she was horribly aware that all eyes were on her.

Sexual harassment isn't just about unwelcome sexual advances. It covers a multitude of circumstances and behaviors that can be construed to explicitly or implicitly affect a person's employment, or that interfere with her or his performance, or that create a hostile or offensive work environment. Wolf whistles, invading a person's space, posting a sexist cartoon, even mocking "courtesy" can be considered sexually harassing if the circumstances, the nature of the behavior, and the context support that charge.

It's all illegal. Unfortunately, proving it in court is expensive, tough to do, and difficult to endure—do you really want details of your office love life put "on the record"? Of course, going to court must be an individual decision based on the facts of the case and the damage alleged. But be aware that at the higher levels of corporate life in particular, the courts have not been all that willing to confirm a finding of harassment and award the plaintiff.

"The problem is very well documented," says Judith Vladeck, a New York attorney who specializes in cases of gender bias and sexual harassment, "but the legal remedy for discrimination against upper-level women in corporate America is not very clear. The courts are unwilling to involve themselves in these situations."

The cause of this unwillingness? Says Vladeck, "When you look at lawsuits over cases where women are denied partnerships or promotions to top ranks, you'll see that the courts really want to keep hands off. They say, essentially, when it comes to issues like upper-level promotions or harassment, that there are many subjective considerations and therefore, they say you have to pay deference to the decision-makers. So we're not getting much help from the courts."

That doesn't mean you should rule out going to court, only that it should be seen as a last resort. The higher your level, the tougher the litigation. It can be a difficult, laborious, long process—with no guarantees at the end.

That being the case, when, if ever, *should* you consult an attorney?

Despite the lack of sympathy from the courts, get legal advice as soon as possible—even if you haven't exhausted all the potential remedies within your organization. Obtaining legal counsel doesn't mean you have to take legal action. Rather, you see a lawyer because you want a better understanding of what's happening to you and what your options are. Remember: Your aim is not just to keep your career, but to keep it on the path toward power.

"It's helpful for a woman to get a lawyer so she doesn't feel she's going it alone," says Vladeck. "Very often, you'll find that women in these situations start questioning themselves and they have very few people they can talk to—few female peers they can discuss the problem with. Lawyers can be useful here just to say, 'Hey, lady, it's not your fault.'

"If you think you're being persecuted, you are. Sometimes, just hearing about what is happening is helpful to a woman."

And a lawyer can help you find a solution short of going to court. Maybe the best move is to file charges but hope to settle out-of-court. Maybe the only thing left to do is actually to opt out—quit the corporation, change jobs, even shift careers and/or leave the corporate world entirely. It's a dismal option, but it may prove your best bet for obtaining the career satisfaction you seek free of harassment and pain.

In any event, it's certainly further confirmation that sex and work don't mix. And it's a sober reminder that you should keep the two pursuits separate—at all times, and at just about all cost.

The bottom line on sex at the office? You think it's not going to be an issue, but it almost always is. The point to remember is that women today have more control than they think. Taking control in this arena, as in just about all others, is the best way to break through to corporate power.

Sex at the office dos and don'ts

- If you are attracted to a colleague, give it some time. Hold off. Don't get in compromising positions until you're really comfortable—until you're sure that what you're feeling is genuine and that there's a good reason to become involved.

- *Don't* show an inordinate amount of attention to an individual if you're in an informal business situation or socializing in a business gathering away from the office. Be sociable, but maintain a distance. Stay in groups. If there's dancing involved, don't dance with just one partner; play the field.

- *Don't* be flattered by unsolicited overtures. You're probably not the first woman that he's hit on, and you won't be the last. Does he have a reputation for office romances? What is his history?

- *Be charming, not cute.* To charm is to please; to be cute is to contrive to be pleasing, without managing to do so genuinely. *Cute* has an edge of seduction; it's aimed toward the opposite sex only and is taken as a signal of romantic intentions. *Charm* is a real quality that can serve women well throughout their careers; it makes everyone around you—men and women alike—more comfortable and positive toward you. Cute really doesn't belong in the corporate boardroom. Charm is welcome anywhere.

- *Don't assume no one will ever find out.* Office relationships are especially hard to conceal, and no communications network is quite as effective as the office grapevine. If you think you've managed to keep your affair a secret, you're probably wrong.

- *Don't dress suggestively.* One corporate VP of our acquaintance insisted on wearing low-cut blouses to work, then complained that men stared at her "inappropriately" and didn't take her seriously. Turned out low-cut, "suggestive" clothing was all she had in her wardrobe. Clearly, she was her own worst enemy, sending a message, whether or not intentionally, that ran completely counter to the formal, businesslike environment in which we're all expected to work. This doesn't mean you have to look prudish or wear unattractive clothing. Dress *appropriately,* and if you're looking for a guide, see what the other successful women in your organization are wearing. They're perfect in-house role models. And finally, if you're wondering whether or not a particular piece of attire is appropriate, leave it in the closet.

- *Do go to higher-ups to get an uncomfortable situation resolved.* If that doesn't work, and if human resources isn't effective—or if seeking HR help is not an option you're comfortable with—*do* seek legal counsel. Fight it, don't accept it. You can't be fired if you talk to a lawyer and seek legal redress. While you should keep in mind that a legal remedy should be a last resort, remember also that you seek legal redress only to confirm your rights, not to ask for special privileges.

STRATEGY 12

Leadership: Be the Lead Dog; It's a Better View

Bill: When women are given responsibility, they have a tendency to act grateful, as if they're in a support role, not someone running the show.

Janice: They're so happy to be at the table, they want to show they can embrace the scope of the responsibility. And of course, if they do act with authority, the old cliché kicks in.

Bill: Which cliché is that?

Janice: The one that says if a man acts with authority, he's assertive; if a woman acts with authority, she's aggressive—or another less favorable term.

Bill: Acting with authority goes with the territory. It's what leaders do.

Janice: Yes, leaders communicate a vision, take risks, and make things happen.

Bill: Women are certainly capable of that—if they would just take the risk!

There's a difference between managing and leading, between control and authority. What difference does the difference make? All

191

the difference in the world. There are plenty of so-called managers in corporate America, and control can be conferred by position in the hierarchy. But unfortunately real leaders are rare, and part of what makes them leaders is the confidence with which they inspire and guide others. "It is the responsibility of the expert to operate the familiar," wrote Henry Kissinger, "and that of the leader to transcend it."

While managing can indeed be artful—keeping tabs carefully, keeping track closely, keeping control tightly to get the job done productively and profitably—there is a real art to leadership—to finding and articulating a fresh path, showing the way, taking the first step, and summoning others to follow. Most American corporations are in fact overmanaged and underled.

Yet corporate America needs both managers and leaders, both control and authority, both execution and vision. When it comes time to hand out corporate power, however, it will go to the leaders whose abilities other people know and trust as proven.

That's why it's important for women who want to assume the mantle of leadership to act with authority and take some risks. "Be the change you want to see," urged Gandhi. You're *ready* for leadership. You've racked up the mileage and the years; you've paid your dues in corporate America. Your achievements thus far have been substantial. Now you're in charge. It's time to start behaving that way. It's time to achieve your leadership destiny.

SCENARIO:

"It is all about 'I am going to get it done,' " says former ITT CFO Ann Reese of her years at Mobil, during the formative stage of her career. "I was simply determined. The idea was that if I could do these things, I could do anything." "These things" included managing the company's finance group in Africa and traveling to Nigeria and other western African destinations at a time when travel there was difficult at best. "I just kept going back, and my staff and I would sit with the Nigerian minister of finance from seven in the morning till seven at night. My eyes would be coated with flies, the heat was terrible, and water wasn't always available, but I was determined to get them to work with us." Once, she was *en route* to the airport when her car was stopped and she was held up at gunpoint. It didn't stop her. When she was seven months pregnant with her second child, she and a staff member were stranded in Sierra Leone. Their airplane back to Lagos was literally in pieces on the runway. Ann climbed over an airport conveyor belt to find—and bribe—some employees to "put the plane back together." She and her associate got back to Nigeria. "Character-forming experiences," she calls them: They showed management qualities of leadership that cannot be learned and are almost impossible to teach. "I wanted to show them," Reese says of her determination. She showed them all right: commitment in action, the ability to lead and coach, the tenacity to pursue a course of action whatever the obstacles.

THATCHER VS. BLAIR

Some people are inherently authoritative. They're the born leaders. Not just the generals and politicians and sometimes the great humanitarians who swayed and shaped their era, but people on smaller stages as well: the kid in school around whom everyone gravitated, the eloquent activist able to stir a crowd, the "natural" captain of the softball team, the rising-star manager who everybody knows is on his or her way to the top.

How does everybody know it? They just do. There's something about him or her that inspires confidence. All things being equal—educational background, age, level of achievement to date—the born leader will still somehow stand out from the pack. It's inherent. You know it when you see it. Just look across the Atlantic for a prime example—actually, a prime ministerial example:

Tony Blair enjoys a bigger majority in the British Parliament than Margaret Thatcher ever dreamed of obtaining. But the hard-nosed "iron lady" simply *exudes* power, self-assurance, the confidence to command. Blair achieved his authority through careful planning, studiously assessing the right strategic moment to bring about radical change in his party, then tactically and charismatically riding the wave of change in his nation. Thatcher was the true believer, the ideologue whose passion percolated almost visibly. Blair seems a delightful guy you'd love to have dinner with. Thatcher seems a force of nature; you may not like her, may not agree with her policies, but you pay attention. Even her own joking about her unofficial title as the Iron Lady of Europe was telling—of course, she had a sense of humor about her power; she could *afford* to.

SIX STEPS

Thatcher or Blair, inherent or achieved, both kinds of leadership ability carry authority.

Can it be simulated? Can leadership ability be fabricated? Can authority be faked? No, but they can be learned—by studying some of the great corporate leaders, modeling their actions, and rehearsing their behaviors. Some good role models? McDonald's visionary Ray Kroc, Wal-Mart's Sam Walton, cosmetics guru Estée Lauder, Disney founder Walt himself, General Electric's Jack Welch, *The Washington Post's* Katherine Graham, and the legendary Alfred Sloan of General Motors—not to mention the leaders who stand out at all levels in your own organization.

"The foundation of effective leadership," wrote management guru Peter F. Drucker, "is thinking through the organization's mission, defining it and establishing it, clearly and visibly. The leader sets the goals, sets the priorities, and sets and maintains the standards."[14] Drucker's words still hold true.

Step 1: Are You a Manager or a Leader?   Are you a manager or a leader? Do you exercise control or command authority? Are you Thatcher or Blair—the natural commander or the one who got there through practice and planning? Take a look at the chart in Figure 12.1 to determine which you are.

Figure 12.1 Manager or Leader.

Manager	Leader
Delegates and investigates issues	Stops "the buck" passing
Listens to the trumpet	Sounds the trumpet
Implements strategies	Creates the vision
Uses resources	Provides resources
Sails the ship	Sets the course
Supports new ideas	Invents, innovates
Evaluates quality	Sets standards
Makes many decisions	Makes few decisions
Builds alliances	Builds trust and integrity
Supports and walks the talk	Articulates the message
Interacts with people	Knows his/her people
Lets people know him/her	Lets people think they know him/her
Gets and delivers feedback	Sets criteria for feedback
Refines current way of doing things	Consistently searches for a better way to do things
Is committed	Is passionately committed

Nine out of ten women reading this book will probably profile themselves as managers, not leaders. That, presumably, is *why* they're reading this book. For while women increasingly are gaining management status, there has been little chance for them to fill leadership positions.

There are lots of reasons one can point to in order to explain this. In their seminal article "Not There Yet," written for *Across the Board,* Dan Dalton and Catherine Daily articulated many of those reasons. But "the long and short of it," Dalton and Daily found, "is that the corporate elite are chosen as a function of their professional and social connections"—and women "are not in positions that provide them with linkages of this type."[15] It is, says one former General Electric exec (female), "a pipeline issue." GE's Jack Welch has himself made a priority of moving women—and minorities—through the pipeline. But, like most corporations, the GE pool from which the GE pipeline can draw women is sparsely populated.

And why is it sparsely populated? We answered that question at the beginning of this book. As every successful woman knows, there's an iron wall holding up the glass ceiling—and it is keeping women out of the ranks of leadership.

Seeing the difference between management and leadership can offer invaluable direction in how to begin to behave like a leader. The idea is to start rehearsing now so that you can step into the top role the moment there's an opening. Here's the rest of the strategy for doing so.

Step 2: Establish and Communicate Clear, Meaningful Goals. Define and articulate your own personal management methodology so that those you hope to lead know exactly what to expect. Put lines across the environment: the boundaries of responsibility, the systems and processes by which you will lead, the lines of communication, your values—for example, what counts in this organization. Be sure you communicate all this throughout your organization.

It's been demonstrated time and again that when people know what is expected of them, they meet or exceed the expectation. The key is to be clear about what the expectations are. People trust more when they know what the deliverables are and when they must be delivered.

Results count, after all. As a leader of people, you will be measured by results; you will measure the people under your leadership by their results. That's why it's so crucial to establish and articulate clear, meaningful goals. It's the only way people will buy in to your program; it's the only way they'll accomplish the tasks you set them.

After all, you want these people to follow you—most likely into new arenas. Give them a map that shows them where they are going, and give them a reason to follow you—a bright, waving banner they can see every step of the way.

Step 3: Build Trust Through Action. How do you get people to follow you into unknown territory? Even more important, how do you get them to follow your command to go into that uncharted territory while you remain behind arranging for resources and support? General Colin Powell has a one-word answer: trust. And how do you achieve trust? Not through florid statements about it, not even through one-on-one discussions. Words are only promises. The confidence in you that is the basis of trust comes only when you demonstrate, in Powell's words, that "you are worthy of their confidence."[16] That means actions. The former chief of staff goes on to cite four kinds of action that demonstrate that you're worthy of the confidence you're asking people to repose in you. These categories of action work as well in business as in the military, and they're our four recommendations as well:

1. Having articulated your expectations and established a timetable, provide the resources and support people needed to do their jobs—for example, the training, equipment, and new information or knowledge.

2. Show people you care about them and their problems by seeking them out and helping them address and resolve any issues they may have. Ask about their problems, so they know they can raise issues freely.

3. Give people recognition—it's the right way to generate and enhance their own feelings of self-worth. Publicly acknowledge their accomplishments through emails, newsletters, lunches.

4. Maintain discipline—including the discipline of getting rid of people who are not doing the job and are thus dragging down the entire organization.

We'll add two more building blocks of *trust*. The first is basic to all the actions you take: Keep open the lines of communication. Essential to that is getting out of the plush office you've earned and checking out the rest of the corridors and cubicles—the haunts of the folks who do the day-to-day work. Some sensitivity and prudence are required here: Doing an unannounced walkabout down among the troops can be a burr under the saddle of your lieutenants and captains. After all, your direct reports have their field of authority as well; it's important to respect that.

On the other hand, it's important to make use of the knowledge of the people on the front line of the business—and that's just the way to position these walkabouts to both those who report to you and those who report to them. Let people know you're going to get out into the real world and cruise the territory. Stop at the offices of the people two and three and four levels down. Knock politely, sit in the available chair, ask for their expertise.

Then make sure you do the same with your direct reports. Meet with them regularly. Listen to them, learn their agenda, find out what they need from you. Let them filter and dilute any raw information you've gleaned right from the line. The more information you have and the more expertise you can get, the wider your own range of options and the more effective your actions. And the more effective your actions, the greater the trust you will build.

The other building block we would add is to keep on teaching your people about leadership itself. Tell them your personal experiences—even your failures—and let them know how you solved dilemmas, came back from defeat, learned from both successes and failures. Let them know you've been where they are now, so that they can relate to your experience and transfer it to what they're dealing with at the moment. This is not about divulging private matters or becoming touchy-feely about your inner core; rather, it's about increasing the comfort level of the people who work for you and with you so that they can learn from you and apply what they've learned.

Step 4: Practice the Competitive Edge, Then Delegate. One very good way to show people you care *and* to recognize their abilities is to delegate responsibility to them. And once you do delegate, give them the resources to do the job, then get out of the way and let them do it. Ronald Reagan said it best: "Surround yourself with the best people you can find, delegate authority, and don't interfere."

The company will keep its competitive edge as long as the people in it keep their competitive edge. It's your job as leader to instill in the team the energy, excellence, execution, and enthusiasm—the four Es—of competitiveness. It may be your most important job and your most valuable contribution as a leader. You'll need to find ways to empower the front line, to challenge the people on the line, then hold them accountable for their actions. You're both coach and facilitator.

While you're the catalyst for change, you need to step aside and let the people of the organization effect the change. Only when people own the problem will they own the solution and make it happen. It's your job as leader to get them to take ownership. Make the connection, but remember that you can only be a model of execution; you can't do it for them.

Sometimes, it's risky. When a project is teetering on the edge of disaster, or a unit of the organization looks to be falling short of its objectives, there's a great temptation to rush in and save the situation—especially since the failure ultimately goes on your record and is something you'll eventually have to deal with. But nobody ever learned to manage by being rescued, and trust cannot be found where none is given. Once you've delegated a task to someone, it ain't your monkey anymore. Step in to offer help, provide support and resources, but let the individual get the monkey off his back himself; it's his or her problem to solve. In other words, show the person the respect you would ask for yourself, and you'll gain the trust you've just demonstrated.

And *your* boss will recognize your own courage and people development skills.

Step 5: The Buck Stops with You. Authority is lonely—no doubt about it. But that is the nature of the beast: The final decision is yours, the final call is up to you. Make sure everyone knows it, and make sure at the same time that everyone knows you value the input they can provide to that final decision-making process.

General Powell told the interviewers of *Context* magazine that he maintained an informal network for information-gathering in addition to the formal network, which, he claimed, tended to give him only what they thought he should know. He made no decision without consulting both networks thoroughly.

As it happens, information-gathering is an area in which women have a real opportunity to make a difference in corporate life. The reason is simple: Women are natural information-gatherers. Their fundamental nurturing instincts empower them to get input from people without intimidation, so that the person offers information and ideas without restraint or restriction, sensing that even the most way-out, wacky ideas will be treated with respect. It means that women have it in their hands to generate more options, more insights, more thoughts and proposals and interpretations—all of which can enrich the decision-making process.

Where women tend to fall short, however, is in gathering more information than may be necessary until analysis paralysis sets in. If you suffer from fear of decision-making, remember this: There's no such thing as having "all the information you need," and there's no decision that can't be altered. Too much input may begin to look like you don't want to make the decision yourself or that you are swayed by the last thing you've heard—and neither impression is a good basis for inspiring trust. Besides, dealing with ambiguity is a certainty for every leader.

Use the strength of your woman's instinct for gathering wide-ranging, creative input. But teach yourself to recognize the moment when you must assume the authority to cut off input, end the debate, and say: "Thanks, all. Now it's up to me."

Step 6: Fill the Title.   You were given the title. It was bestowed on you. How will you fill it? Will you see it as a reward for past achievements, a level of authority you've earned and can exercise because the HR man-

200

ual says you can? Or will you regard it as an opportunity to practice the exercise of the ultimate power you seek—a rehearsal for serious senior leadership?

Obviously, we think you should see it as the latter—an opportunity for practicing power and rehearsing leadership. To do that, you must shift your mind-set. Remember how you always used to look up to the leader in the organization? You're the leader now. Accept yourself as such. Stop second-guessing yourself as "Corporate Woman"; start behaving as Corporate Leader.

Of course, when you say "Charge!" you want to be sure the people who look up to you as leader are out in front taking the hill. That's how you get results and bring benefit to the organization. That's how you make the organization better off *because of your leadership*. And that is the point of the matter. Simply put: It is not healthy for a leader to have unhappy stockholders.

You're not there to be loved by the people you lead—although that is always a nice by-product. You're there to run the organization. There's no requirement to show gratitude or defensiveness; the only requirement is to succeed. Leadership can be a most becoming and most satisfying garment. Wear it with authority.

TIPS ON BEING A LEADER/ SHOWING AUTHORITY

1. Boldness takes leaders where others fear to tread. Be a risk-taker with the self-confidence to make it work—if not at first, then on the second try, or the third . . .

2. You can't please all of the people all of the time. If you don't show you're capable of taking the unpopular stand, you can lose people's faith in you as a leader.

3. Remember that authority is bestowed, power is taken. Take more than usual and look for greater authority.

4. Encourage subordinates to present their views, argue with you, offer input. Let them spread the word that they "argued with

the boss" and helped the boss come to a decision. It's good for both your reputations.

5. Take the credit and share the credit, but always keep the blame.

6. Do not be private about your values. Let it be known that forthrightness, honesty, and integrity are prized. Be trustworthy.

7. Communicate. Then communicate again. Then communicate once more. Then walk around and listen.

8. Hire, train, retain, promote, and recognize all your people according to their abilities and willingness to contribute. Share your war stories, and be there to coach them toward success.

9. Build a cadre of talent to replace you; create a self-sustaining unit/company.

10. Assume the perspective of a team member. It can offer important insights.

11. Be a visionary—and articulate the big-picture sense of purpose for others.

12. Demonstrate positive thinking, enthusiasm, and a spirit that can inspire others.

13. Stick to your course of action. If you shift with the winds, the people following you will grow dizzy.

14. Be inner-directed: Show that you know who you are and are comfortable with where you stand and where you're going.

15. Question the status quo. Challenge assumptions. Be ideational.

Woman to Woman

"Since it was founded more than 25 years ago as a graduate school of business for women only, the program at Simmons College has continued to grow even as women have gained greater acceptance at the major mainstream M.B.A. programs. Today the description for the management and behavior course still promises students a lesson in the 'dominance of male norms' and the 'dismissal of female values' in the workplace.

"But with so many women having broken through the barriers that once held them back, Simmons administrators have a new goal: to groom women for advanced leadership roles as chief executives. That will not happen by teaching women simply to mimic men in the boardroom, says Simmons' Professor Fletcher; 'We've been reading those books for 30 years.'

"Instead, she suggests aspiring women executives should act not like men, or even women, but individuals with their own leadership qualities. Patricia O'Brien, Dean of the school, calls it 'finding their voice.' "[17]

Today, successful businesswomen are not just finding but are also sharing their voice.

The scene is The Breakers in Palm Beach, Florida, the lavish five-star resort in the world's most legendary winter paradise. You enter the century-old main building to find yourself surrounded by richly colored paintings of Renaissance noblemen and rulers. Spectacular Venetian chandeliers sparkle, and the ceilings, hand-painted by Florentine artists, are flecked with gold leaf.

Balancing this Augustan elegance are state-of-the-art amenities, the latest and the best of everything, from the four oceanfront pools, to the fitness center with ocean view, to the championship golf course and ten tennis courts, to the luxury spa where guests are richly pampered in both body and soul.

For corporate conference participants, The Breakers is the top of the line. You can just picture it, can't you? Corporate princes, the spiritual descendants of all those noble potentates in all those paintings, plot their mergers and acquisitions, their re-engineerings and reorganizations, during a morning golf game . . . or over lunch at The Beach Club, with the soft breezes from the Atlantic whispering through the royal palms . . . or at The Reef Bar after a hard tennis match . . . or while getting a facial at The Spa. . . .

A facial at The Spa? What's wrong with this picture?

In a world in which women take their rightful place beside men at the heads of corporations, there is less and less wrong with this picture. In fact, the picture comes to us as the brainchild of one of corporate America's most powerful leaders, Heidi G. Miller. Miller, onetime Travelers Group whiz kid and numbers-cruncher *extraordinaire,* former Citigroup CFO, and former *Priceline.com* CFO, founded Women and Co., a conference of 150 top female executives, the precise group for which facials-and-financials is no anomaly, but is, rather, what you do at a meeting of powerful colleagues.

Miller is not alone in looking for some sort of structure to support and advance women in power in corporations. There's Betsy Holden's Working Mom's Exchange Network, a support group Holden formed at Kraft long before she became its CEO. There's JoAnn Heffernan-Heisen's Women's Leadership Initiative at Johnson

& Johnson, created, says Heffernan-Heisen, "to get women out of staff and into line positions." There's Bravo Networks' President Kathy Dore, who made herself a mentor to a young VP at a rival company and helped her rise in the industry.

Sadly, however, these women are the exception rather than the rule. In fact, one of the unhappiest observations we bring to the writing of this book is that women who rise to power in American corporations seem to feel little responsibility toward the women coming up behind them. Virtually all the women we interviewed cited this woman-on-woman prejudice, and all found it unfortunate.

"From my experience," says consultant Marilyn Puder-York, "women are not automatically supportive of other women." It is, says Jewell Bickford, "the saddest part of the story."

How to account for it? There are several reasons. Some have to do with how women connect or disconnect with each other, how they approach other women for help. For some women, it is a zero-sum game: My gain is your loss, your gain is my loss. Other women who have "made it," like many men at the top, have succumbed to the seductive culture of corporate narcissism, what Alan Downs in *Beyond the Looking Glass*[18] defines as "obsession with the image of success." Corporate narcissism, says Downs, derives from the individual narcissistic manager whose only goal is to maintain the aura on the way up the corporate ladder, richly rewarding those who contribute to his or her prestige and sacrificing anyone and anything to gratify the ego. It leaves little room for helping others to climb up the ladder after you.

SCENARIO:

Harriet and Mary worked together at a renowned financial services organization. They respected each other; each considered the other a friend. With Harriet in line for a key position, Mary was asked by their common boss what she thought of her pal. In fact, Mary believed Harriet to be an effective manager who could grow into and succeed in the position, but the way the boss posed the question gave her pause. "I don't really think Harriet has the right stuff for this position," the boss had said, "but I thought I'd ask your opinion." Her political antennae aroused, Mary hedged in her support for Harriet, neither praising her nor precisely blaming her, but leaving the boss with the impression that she shared his assessment.

A month later, the boss was fired. One of his last acts was to let it be known that Mary had not supported Harriet for the new position, which Harriet had obtained and in which she was succeeding admirably. As life would have it, Harriet was soon appointed to head the entire division. She was aware, of course, that her "friend" Mary had not supported or helped her rise to power. She took no action and said not a word, but Mary eventually left the organization. In her own eyes, she had failed in an important responsibility as a corporate woman—the responsibility to stand up for other women at this stage in women's progress. She had chosen short-term political expediency over speaking her true mind and helping a talented colleague and friend. She had gained nothing; she had lost a colleague and friend, her place in the organization (and a step in her career development), and a good deal of her self-respect.

THE FIRST WOMEN UP THE LADDER

For the first generation of women leaders, promoting other women was clearly not a top priority. Understandably so: What drove these women was the desire to run in the men's race, not to pave the way for other women. They were playing a men's game in which the enemy was not just the guys but also the other women trying to enter through the same narrow door.

Today, women's associations like Heidi Miller's Women and Co. exhibit a more supportive sharing of experiences and information— at least from industry to industry and corporation to corporation.

Inside the organization, however, women still often stand alone and aloof from one another. The competition to get to the top is still there, and it's still a fierce fight for a rare resource. All's fair in love, war, and getting to the top. For many women, this is reason enough to just cut another woman out of the picture, even a friend. After all, isn't that what men do?

THE SECOND GENERATION OF CORPORATE WOMEN

As it turns out, the picture is not much different among the post–baby boomers who today constitute the "second generation" of corporate women, although their reasons for not helping other women may be different. Many don't see the need to reach out to other women, as Janice learned when she posed a question to a panel of women business leaders, all from the e-business world, at *Fortune* magazine's 1999 50 Most Powerful Women Conference in New York City. To the question, "What are you doing to support and promote women at your company or at the companies on whose boards you sit?" the answer was that the point was moot. The new economy offers "a level playing field," the e-woman replied; there's "no prejudice"; "if you are good," you will make it.

Our research suggests otherwise. Just ask Heidi Miller. Once the most powerful woman at Citigroup, Miller left the venerable financial institution to join Priceline.com as chief financial officer. She resigned less than a year later, citing a disinclination to be part of "a workout situation . . . at this time in my career." Miller asserted that she had not soured on dot-coms; rather, her disillusion was with the idea that Internet start-ups would be more welcoming to women. But Miller found cyberspace executives just as inhospitable as button-down executives. "I don't think young men are any less biased than old men are," Miller said in a *New York Times* interview.[1] Where bias against women is concerned, Miller went on, "dot-coms are smaller versions of big corporations." In short the handwriting is on the wall even in the new Internet companies, where the organizational structure is becoming increasingly hierarchical and—astonishingly—where women are finding that even cyberspace may be a men's club. Who heads the most successful e-businesses? As experienced talent is brought in from the old economy companies to run or advance these start-ups, women on the way up may not hold on to the power they have managed to attain thus far.

Yet another issue for women, according to those interviewed for this book, is sheer exhaustion. After so much time and effort spent getting to the position of power, who has the time or energy to help others? And, not to put too fine a point on it, why open to competitors a door nobody opened to you?

WHY HELP WOMEN?

One possible answer is the one Louis Armstrong gave when someone asked him to explain jazz. "If you gotta ask," Satchmo replied with his signature grin, "you ain't never gonna know."

Corporate women will only really be successful when more women are making the strategic decisions in corporations, and to get to that point, women need to call on other women to "close the deal" just as men call on other men. The best analogy is the example of how little attention was given to women's health issues until the number of women in Congress increased; only then did women's health get the attention and focus it needed. Similarly, it may not be until women are a natural presence in corporate boardrooms that women will enjoy full equality of opportunity in corporate America. That's one good reason to help other women; in doing so, you help all women— including your daughter and granddaughter!

But the ultimate reason to help other women rise as you have risen in the corporate world is because it's good business. The business case for diversity in corporate leadership is by now well established. It's a diverse world, and women make up a huge portion of it. If your company's customers don't see anybody from your company who looks like them, they may assume that the company doesn't really speak their language and cannot really understand their needs. And they will probably be right. You owe it to your own company's future—as well as to other women in the corporation—to extend a helping hand to competent evolved women who could rise faster with your support.

BEND THE RULES

Yet for women who've worked as hard as you have, who've struggled relentlessly to stand out from the pack, paid their dues, labored to lay the political groundwork, honed their skills and broadened their perspective, it still somehow feels like cheating to give what sounds like favored treatment to anyone else, much less on the basis of gender. Moreover, what happens if you help a fellow woman and she turns out not to be very good? Won't it reflect on you?

When Ann Reese was CFO of ITT, she went out on a limb specifically on women's issues. She wasn't necessarily out to change company policy for all women, but rather to help select individuals, those who were top performers, by bending the rules.

It didn't always work out, but it didn't stop Reese from helping women, from hiring them, developing them, and promoting them. "That wouldn't be fair," Reese says. "And it wouldn't have been good business. After all, business sometimes requires risk-taking, and while not every risk works out, that goes for men and for women. Didn't anyone ever give you a break? Didn't you ever need one?" The point is: As someone with power, you have the opportunity—and the resources—to give a break to the next person. And as someone seeking power and in need of a break, you have a perfect right to ask for one.

A RIGHT AND A WRONG WAY
TO ASK FOR HELP

"Women often approach things as either entitled princesses or victims," says Dr. Marilyn Puder-York, "but for the evolved women that is too much of a burden."

Women cannot ask other women for help just because they share the same gender. Corporate women are busy. Corporate women in positions of leadership and power are particularly busy. The last thing they need is to spend time with someone who just wants to come in and touch the hem of their garment. "Hi, I'm calling to network" is the kiss of death if you're trying to approach these women. "Can I explore how you got where you are?" or "Just wondering if you have any wisdom about what your industry is like" or "I hoped we could just chat for a minute or two" are all calculated to make the person tune out and turn off. Hardly the result you want. Rather, evolved women want to help women who have done their homework.

Moreover, corporate women with power conserve the resources that power gives them—and so they should. It doesn't mean they will not take a chance with some of those resources, but it also doesn't mean they will toss the resources down a black hole. So if you are going to ask for help—a recommendation for a job, for example— make sure that you are qualified for that job. If you are asking for someone's imprimatur on a report or study, make sure that report or study is in final-final draft, with every fact and figure checked, with a clean, crisp summary of findings and a clear, well-developed set of recommendations. In other words, when you ask for help, deserve it. Don't waste a busy woman's time.

And whatever you're asking for, make sure your request is specific and highly focused. Know your facts. Anticipate the questions you might be asked, and prepare your answers. Be brief. Use the person's time with respect. And be sure to say thank you by word, by note, or by an invitation to a wonderful event. They may be too busy to attend, but your thoughtfulness will be recognized. And remember successful women do not and should not squander their time needlessly.

USE YOUR POWER—BRING MORE WOMEN TO YOUR TABLE

What are you afraid of? Do you fear the same-sex competition men have been dealing with for years? Are you afraid that other women will outshine you? Are you afraid of losing your position—one you relish—as the only woman at the table?

If you're tempted to push for day care because you can see that your organization would benefit from it, are you afraid people will say you're an advocate for women's issues? So? What's wrong with being an advocate for women's issues if they make good business sense?

If a worthy woman in your employ needs time to spend with a sick child or a sick parent, are you afraid people will whisper that women "bend the rules for women"? Has no man in power in a corporation ever bent the rules for a man who needed to attend to a sick child?

If you have to decide between two equally qualified outside vendors, are you afraid to choose the woman because people will say you're biased? And: Did nobody in a corporation ever give business to a member of *his* club?

Power is there to be used. That's the great lesson awaiting women as they rise to power in corporate America. It should be used to change policies and practices. It should be used to take a risk on someone. It should be used to fill the pocketbooks and build the power of people too long kept from power.

As a woman who has reached the inner sanctum of corporate

power, you have a sphere of influence within which your decisions can make a difference—for your company, for yourself, and for other individuals. Remember how it was for you when you were on the hunt for the big game? Use the power you have to help the women gunning for power now. That's what power is all about. Make a difference, change history, and help make women with the power the norm in corporate America. It's not up to them; it's up to us.

Notes

1. Statistics in this chapter come from Catalyst, the research and advisory organization that provides invaluable data on women in business. www.catalystwomen.org.
2. "Women and Minorities Continue to Take a Back Seat in Business," by Pepi Sappal. *Wall Street Journal*, October 17, 2000.
3. "Study Says Women Face Glass Walls as Well as Ceilings," by Julie Amparano Lopez, *Wall Street Journal*, March 3, 1991.
4. "The 50 Most Powerful Women in Business," by Patricia Sellers. *Fortune*, October 16, 2000.
5. *New York Times*, May 26, 2000.
6. Morin, William J. *Total Career Fitness*. San Francisco: Jossey-Bass, 2000.
7. *The American Heritage Dictionary of the English Language, Third Edition*. Houghton Mifflin Company, 1992.
8. Many leave the corporation at this point and open their own businesses. In fact, the National Foundation for Women Business Owners found that the number of women-owned businesses in the United States has more than doubled during the past twelve years. The reason? According to the Foundation and Catalyst, 22 percent of those women who formed businesses cited a corporate "glass ceiling" as one reason they entered the entrepreneurial world.

9. Welch quotes from "Taking a Break." *Business Week,* June 8, 1998.

10. Downs, Alan. *Beyond the Looking Glass.* New York: Amacom, 1997.

11. *Wall Street Journal.*

12. Briles, Judith. *Gendertraps: Confronting Confrontophobia, Toxic Bosses, and Other Landmines at Work.* New York: McGraw-Hill, 1996.

13. "Listening Is the Secret Behind Art of Talk," by Morey Stettner, *Investor's Business Daily,* February 10, 2000.

14. "Leadership: More Doing Than Dash" by Peter F. Drucker, *Wall Street Journal,* January 6, 1988.

15. "Not There Yet," by Dan R. Dalton and Catherine M. Daily, *Across the Board,* November/December, 1998.

16. "Follow the Leader: Gen. Colin Powell explains how to inspire people to achieve even more than they imagined possible," *Context,* February-March 2000.

17. "Beyond the Glass Ceiling: Women's MBA Program Is Redefining Its Mission," *New York Times,* August 30, 2000.

18. Downs, Alan. *Beyond the Looking Glass: Overcoming the Seductive Culture of Corporate Narcissism.* New York: Amacom, 1997.

19. Executive Assesses Her Adventure At a Dot-Com," by Patrick McGeehan. *New York Times,* November 9, 2000.

References and Resources

The following organizations and periodicals provided data used in the writing of this book:

Catalyst
120 Wall Street
New York, NY 10005

The National Foundation for Women Business Owners (NFWBO)
1411 K Street, NW, Suite 1350
Washington, DC 20005-3407

Context magazine (contextmag.com)

Fast Company magazine (fastcompany.com)

Investor's Business Daily

The New York Times

The Wall Street Journal

In addition, the following may provide useful insight:

Axtell, Roger E.; Briggs, Tami; Corcoran, Margaret; Lamb, Mary Beth. *Do's and Taboos Around the World for Women in Business.* John Wiley & Sons, New York, 1997.

Benton, D. A. *Secrets of a CEO Coach: Your Personal Training Guide to Thinking Like a Leader and Acting like a CEO.* McGraw-Hill, New York, 1999.

Blanke, Gail. *In My Wildest Dreams: Living the Life You Long For.* Simon & Schuster, New York, 1998.

Briles, Judith. *Gender Traps: Conquering Confrontophobia, Toxic Bosses and Other Landmines at Work.* McGraw-Hill, New York, 1996.

Brooks, Donna, and Lynn Brooks. *Seven Secrets of Successful Women: Success Strategies of the Women Who Have Made It—and How You Can Follow Their Lead.* McGraw-Hill, New York, 1997.

Cameron, Julia, and Mark Bryan. *The Artist's Way: A Spiritual Path to Higher Creativity.* J. P. Tarcher, New York, 1992.

Carr-Ruffino, Norma, Ph.D. *The Promotable Woman: 10 Essential Skills for the New Millennium.* Career Press, Franklin Lakes, NJ, 1997.

Catalyst. *Advancing Women in Business, the Catalyst Guide, Best Practices from the Corporate Leaders.* Jossey-Bass, San Francisco, 1998.

Downs, Alan. *Beyond the Looking Glass: Overcoming the Seductive Culture of Corporate Narcissism.* Amacom, New York, 1997.

Elgin, Suzette Haden. *The Gentle Art of Verbal Self-Defense.* Barnes & Noble, New York, 1980.

Evans, Gail. *Play Like a Man, Win Like a Woman: What Men Know About Success That Women Need to Learn.* Broadway Books, New York, 2000.

Felder, Deborah G. *A Century of Women: The Most Influential Events in 20th Century Women's History.* Carol Publishing, Secaucus, NJ, 1999.

Fisher, Helen. *The First Sex: Natural Talents of Women and How They Are Changing the World.* Random House, New York, 1999.

Flaherty, Tina Santi. *Talk Your Way to the Top: The Savviest Book on Communication Ever Written for Women*. A Perigee Book, New York, 1999.

Fox, Jeffrey J. *How to Become CEO: The Rules for Rising to the Top of Any Organization*. Hyperion, New York, 1998.

Frenier, Carol R. *Business and the Feminine Principle: The Untapped Resource*. Butterworth-Heinemann, Woburn, MA, 1997.

Gallagher, Carol, Ph.D. *Going to the Top: A Road Map for Success from America's Leading Women Executives*. Viking Penguin, New York, 2000.

Gilberd, Pamela Boucher. *The Eleven Commandments of Wildly Successful Women*. Macmillan Spectrum, New York, 1996.

Glaser, Connie, and Barbara Steinberg Smalley. *Swim with the Dolphins: How Women Can Succeed in Corporate America on Their Own Terms*. Warner Books, New York, 1995.

Harrison, Patricia. *A Seat at the Table: An Insiders Guide for America's New Women Leaders*. MasterMedia, New York, 1994.

Helgesen, Sally. *Everyday Revolutionaries: Working Women and the Transformation of American Life*. Doubleday, New York, 1998.

Hyatt, Carole, and Linda Gottlieb. *When Smart People Fail: Rebuilding Yourself for Success*. Penguin Books, New York, revised edition 1993.

Jamieson, Kathleen Hall. *Beyond the Double Bind: Women and Leadership*. Oxford University Press, New York, 1995.

Jones, Constance. *1001 Things Everyone Should Know About Women's History*. Doubleday, New York, 1998.

McKenna, Elizabeth Perle. *When Work Doesn't Work Anymore: Women, Work and Identity*. Delacorte Press, New York, 1997.

Mendell, Adrienne, M.A. *How Men Think: The Seven Essential Rules for Making It in a Man's World.* Ballantine Books, New York, 1996.

Morin, William J. *Total Career Fitness: A Complete Checkup and Work-out Guide.* Jossey-Bass, San Francisco, 2000.

Morrison, Ann M., Randall P. White, Ellen Van Velsor, and the Center for Creative Leadership. *Breaking the Glass Ceiling: Can Women Reach the Top of America's Largest Corporations?* Addison-Wesley, Boston, 1992.

Moses, Barbara, Ph.D. *Career Intelligence: The 12 New Rules for Work and Life Success.* Berrett-Koehler Publishers, Inc., San Francisco, 1997.

Neff, Thomas J., and James M. Citrin. *Lessons from the Top: The Search for America's Best Business Leaders.* Currency Doubleday, New York, 1999.

Nichols, Nancy A., ed. *Reach for the Top: Women and the Changing Facts of Work Life.* A Harvard Business Review Book, 1994.

O'Brien, Virginia. *Success on Our Own Terms: Tales of Extraordinary, Ordinary Business Women.* John Wiley and Sons, New York, 1998.

Rubin, Harriet. *The Princessa: Machiavelli for Women.* Dell, New York, 1997.

Salmansohn, Karen. *How to Succeed in Business Without a Penis: Secrets and Strategies for the Working Woman.* Three Rivers Press, New York, 1996.

Shaevitz, Marjorie Hansen. *The Confidant Woman: Learn the Rules of the Game.* Harmony Books, New York, 1999.

Slater, Robert. *Get Better or Get Beaten: 31 Leadership Secrets from GE's Jack Welch.* McGraw-Hill, New York, 1994.

Swiss, Deborah J. *Women Breaking Through: Overcoming the Final 10 Obstacles at Work.* Peterson's/Pacesetter Books, New Jersey, 1996.

Vinnicombe, Susan, and Nina L. Colwill. *The Essence of Women in Management.* Prentice Hall, United Kingdom, 1995.

Weiner, Edith, and Arnold Brown. *Office Biology, or Why Tuesday Is Your Most Productive Day and Other Relevant Facts for Survival in the Workplace.* MasterMedia, New York, 1993.

Wesman, Jane. *Dive Right In, The Sharks Won't Bite: The Entrepreneurial Woman's Guide to Success.* Prentice Hall, Upper Saddle River, NJ, 1995.

White, Kate. *Why Good Girls Don't Get Ahead But Gutsy Girls Do: 9 Secrets Every Working Woman Must Know.* Warner Books, New York, 1997.

Index